A WALK BESIDE ME

A WALK BESIDE ME

DEANN HUMMEL

iUniverse LLC
Bloomington

A WALK BESIDE ME

iUniverse books may be ordered through booksellers or by contacting:

iUniverse LLC
1663 Liberty Drive
Bloomington, IN 47403
www.iuniverse.com
1-800-Authors (1-800-288-4677)

Because of the dynamic nature of the Internet, any web addresses or links contained in this book may have changed since publication and may no longer be valid. The views expressed in this work are solely those of the author and do not necessarily reflect the views of the publisher, and the publisher hereby disclaims any responsibility for them.

Any people depicted in stock imagery provided by Thinkstock are models, and such images are being used for illustrative purposes only. Certain stock imagery © Thinkstock.

ISBN: 978-1-4917-2477-4 (sc)
ISBN: 978-1-4917-2479-8 (hc)
ISBN: 978-1-4917-2478-1 (e)

Library of Congress Control Number: 2014902755

Printed in the United States of America.

iUniverse rev. date: 02/12/2014

The story is dedicated to the loving memory of
Luke William Hummel.

Our son lived his life to the fullest, always with a smile on his face.
In a short period of time, he touched so many people's lives.
He taught us to let go of the little things that didn't matter
and grab hold of what really matters, and that is love!

Luke had plenty of the real, unconditional love that God intended us all to have. There is something we all fail to do but need to, and that is be good to one another, care for one another, help one another. We need to forgive one another, and most of all, we need to love one another.

God loves each one of us equally, and what he does for one he will do for another. In God's eyes, we are divine just the way we are. He made each one of us unique in every way possible. He is not surprised about you. He loves you just the way you are.

We need to sit up and take notice before it is too late to share our love with others. Show others the real you, the one deep inside who no one gets to see because of all the walls you have built to keep yourself locked in safe and sound . . . or so you think. That way of thinking is so far off base it only causes more heartache and pain to you and those around you.

When you are full of bitterness and sorrow and anger, you go around wearing your pain on your sleeve, not realizing we all have been hurt at one time or another. There is a time in your life when you have to let things go, let all the walls come down, and let all the love in. It's the best medicine you can take to get past all your mistakes and regrets. The time is now to let in love.

As I wrote this book, I started listening to my heart a little more closely, and slowly God showed me all the walls I had put up around myself. He told me I needed to let go and trust him and he would see me through. The first step was to let his love in, and as I did that, the walls of pain began to fall around me. I began to see life in a different light. I began to see love in a grander way, just as Luke saw it and lived it. Throughout Luke's life, he taught us what love really meant by living it, not just saying the word. He had the actions to back it up.

How you treat someone is more important than what you do for him or her. It means more. Think about it. What does love really mean to you? When you have love in your heart, you have peace and joy. Love with your heart and not your head. Your head puts conditions on love, but your heart does not.

Don't miss out on encouraging others along the way. That's something you want to be a part of. Enjoy every moment of your journey. Share love with those who cross your path. Let the hurt of yesterday go, and fill your heart with love today. Remember, it's all about God and all the love he gives to each of us.

Thank you, Luke, for all the love you gave and the example you lived. Words cannot express how much you have blessed us. We love and miss you. You are exactly where you want to be. You ran your race right into Jesus' arms. God bless you, and enjoy every moment. We will see you again someday.

Love, Mom and Dad, Latisha and Auston, family and friends

CONTENTS

INTRODUCTION

This book is about one special boy who touched so many lives by the way he lived. There was no need to complain; he knew where his journey was taking him and where he was going. When his turn came up and his name was called, he knew his race was won.

Right from the start, he never gave up. He always had a positive attitude and outlook on life, and he wasn't afraid to share it with others. He lived it. He loved and was a blessing to everyone he met and knew. He spread the fruit of love along the way as he shared it with others.

He brought us trust, joy, forgiveness, learning, fun, faith, hope, determination, and, most of all, love. Even when you didn't deserve it, he loved you anyway. He endured throughout his life with grace, mercy, and patience.

Luke, you did the best you could, and that's all that matters. I give myself permission to keep moving forward. Thank you for being my son and loving me the way you did, just the way you did for me. Don't be afraid; God and I will be with you every step of the way. Start today and do what is in your heart.

We all complain when we have to wait a little while. But we have no reason to complain—we need to be more grateful and thankful for everything we have been given, instead of complaining about what we don't have or isn't coming fast enough. Take a look around and see what others have no control over. They have every reason to complain, and it's amazing they choose not to. And we have no reason to complain, but we do anyway, without a second thought. I've done it myself; we all have.

Listen to yourself; hear what you say. Make an attitude adjustment. A positive outlook makes everything a little brighter and lighter than before. Keep hoping and believing, and new dreams will follow.

I've learned more from being Luke's mother than I ever did from any textbook. We learn more from the things we experience in life than from someone telling us how to experience it. We gain more wisdom through each and every test and trial we face—especially the ones where we have no idea what lies ahead or what's coming right around the corner.

Each trial and tribulation is like a stepping-stone you need to cross—to learn from it and take from it, for your own good. While you are wading through the rapids, you don't know why. But just remember, there is always a reason. When the time is right, you'll know it. Each thing you go through, you're not being punished; you're supposed to learn and grow from it.

Life is a journey; each day you learn something new that you didn't know the day before. Have fun and live life to the fullest. Experience all the joy life has to offer. Enjoy every step of the way. Look at life as our kids do, with not a worry in their world, because they know that they will be taken care of by their heavenly father.

Throughout Luke's life, we allowed him to go his own way. He chose the way he wanted to go. If he was up to it, he was able to experience a lot of the things he wanted to. God doesn't set limits on our dreams; we are the ones who put limits on ourselves and our growth. God wants us to experience all the desires he has put in each one of our hearts.

That is why each day brings a new experience with God. He wants to be with us every step of the way, to help us learn and grow and experience everything together. Once we begin to set limits on ourselves, we stay stuck in a rut with no gut. We are unable to grow and reach the dreams that were placed in our hearts. Once we take the walls down, our limits are lifted.

Step out and take a leap of faith, and you will begin to grow once again. The light will begin to shine bright down deep in your soul. The real you will show up and take notice. You will begin to realize and see what life is all about—how precious life is, and how we must enjoy every moment as a gift. We need to share love; this is the part of the gift to give to others.

Looking back on Luke's journey, he had a lot of courage, strength, and love to go around, and he shared that love with everyone he met along the way. He wasn't afraid to be himself. He was humble in every way possible. He treated everyone equal and just as they were.

It took a lot of courage and strength to get up with a smile on his face every day, even when he was in pain. He never complained and was always more concerned about others than him self. He always noticed something new about you, such as what you were wearing or a new haircut. Luke would let you know if it looked good or not, always with you in mind.

He would notice even if you'd moved the furniture around. Even the little things others would overlook, he would notice. He cared about the little things. Everything mattered to him—no matter how big or small, it all mattered. He could see the whole picture while others couldn't see what he saw and know the reason.

For those who didn't get to meet Luke and know what a blessing he was, I hope that this book will give you a picture of how special he was to those who knew and loved him. There is not a day that goes by that we don't think of Luke and his smiling face that touched so many lives in such a short time.

The whole time we thought we were teaching Luke, he was actually teaching and blessing us. Luke fulfilled his destiny and purpose. He lived life to the fullest and always with a smile on his face; spreading joy along the way to everyone he met. We all received a front-row seat to a glimpse of heaven. Luke was a window to God right in front of us as we look back over his life. He never gave up, and he always had a positive attitude. Luke was joyful. He trusted and was quick to forgive; he had forgiveness in his heart from the start.

Learn to let go of your anger. The only person you are hurting is yourself and no one else. Once you understand that concept, God will take what has angered you and make it right again. You have to trust him and keep moving forward each day.

Share love and happiness with others. Keep your faith alive, keep your hope alive, stay determined to learn, and take what life throws at you. It is actually teaching you something that you need to learn to take with you, and learning is fun. Most of all, share lots of love with others unconditionally, just as God loves us. He loves you just the way you are. Accept everyone as they are. You're not the judge—it's the Lord's job, not yours or mine.

God knows what needs to be done. He will get it done. He sees and hears everything, and it will be done. You do your part, he'll do his part. God loves you, and you are special in every way. Keep believing in your hope and new dreams to follow.

Remember God's promise that he whispers to you in your heart: *The sun always comes up tomorrow. It is brighter than the day before and the day before that. Open your heart; let the love in.* As you read this, read with an open heart, and you will begin to understand.

Every child is special, and that includes you. Look and see what a wonderful place it would be if we all shared love with each other. It can start with just one, with you or me. It starts with one love and grows from there.

CHAPTER 1

The Beginning

One fine day, a boy came to the door and rang the bell. A shy little girl answered. The boy asked if her brother was home. He wanted to see if her brother was going to play football that year at school. She answered, "I don't know," and slammed the door in the boy's face.

As fate would have it, their paths would cross again five years later. At that time, my parents owned a bar, and George and his wife came in on Friday nights. We all hung out on weekends, and George and I were introduced to each other once again—the boy at the door and the little sister. This time, we became friends.

Have you ever wondered why some people stay together and some don't? Only God knows why. George and his wife did not stay together. When I heard about that, I thought that George was a nice person. I wasn't sorry he was single again.

You know how you pray for something to come your way? That was one of those times. I had been praying for God to send me someone special. My prayers came true when God whispered in my ear and said, "Look, he is right in front of you. If you want my gift, go for it, it is yours for the taking."

I took a leap of faith and jumped in with both feet. I knew it was going to take some time. I knew in my heart it would be worth the wait. I wanted to let him know that I was different from other girls he had known—because we belonged together, even though others thought different. Once you keep your faith and focus on what God has planned for you, there is nothing standing in your way. As time went by, the more our love grew stronger . . . and the more my family didn't approve of him.

The summer came to a close, and a new school year began. Homecoming was right around the corner. The football game was in the afternoon, and the dance was in the evening. George knew I really wanted to go, but the only way I would be able to attend was if we had permission. George went right to my front door and got permission from my parents. We were thrilled when they said yes.

My mom took me shopping to get a new dress for the dance. It was so beautiful. I couldn't wait for George to see me in it.

The day finally arrived. It took me a little while to get ready for the evening. My dad couldn't believe it was the same girl who a few hours before was in tennis shoes and blue jeans. I wanted to be perfect in every way possible.

George came to the house to pick me up. He was wearing a blue tailored suit. I was in a lacy dress. We looked like we stepped off the front cover of a magazine. He brought me flowers for my dress and some for his suit.

Everything was amazing, especially how everything was falling together for our evening. It was so special; it was like I was floating on air. We had a great time. We had so many compliments that evening. There was a gentleman who even thought we had just gotten married.

My family thought that after the dance was over, it would be the last of us. Wrong. It only made our love stronger. I know now that my family just wanted the best for me, to make sure I would not get hurt. But the more they tried to keep us apart, the more it backfired.

That summer, my sister had a baby and needed help after she got home from the hospital. So I went down to help her with the new baby. I wasn't able to leave word with George about where I was going until I got down to my sister's house to use her phone. I didn't want him to think I just up and left and he wouldn't see me again.

After we talked, George told me he had a surprise. We made plans to get together at the next softball game. Once the game was over, we met up at the high-school football field so he could give me my surprise. George pulled out a box that held a ring with turquoise stones and a silver band. It was beautiful—I loved it! It was a promise ring. He loved me and wanted to be with me.

George introduced me to his parents, and they thought I was so young that I needed to show them my driver's license to prove my age. I felt very welcome in their home. His parents were very nice.

We spent a lot of time together throughout the softball season, since we shared the same mitt and played the same position. We got to watch each other play. Our love grew stronger and stronger every day. We wanted to spend every moment together.

When it is young love, nothing else seems to matter but each other. You take a leap of faith, and there's no turning back once a decision has been made to move forward. As long as we were together, we could face what we needed to face. You know in your heart that the decision you made is not going to be easy, but you do it anyway, not knowing what lies ahead or the curves that are in front of you. Looking out for the best is the box you are about to walk out of, to take the first step into uncharted territory you have never seen.

One hot summer night, a seed was planted. Each day it grew and grew. Our love had blossomed into something real. In time, we knew how real it was—when I began to show as the blossom grew from the seed planted on that summer night under the moonlight. From that day forward, our hearts were filled with faith and a can-do attitude. We had no idea what lay ahead of us, but we knew for sure we loved each other. That was all we needed to know.

What tomorrow may bring is up to the stars and the morning light and the heaven shining bright in our hearts tonight.

CHAPTER 2

Moving Out

It was the beginning of my eleventh-grade school year. All I could keep my mind on was the summer George and I had shared and all the fun we had, all the love our hearts had spoken that we knew was going to last. We knew we were going to have obstacles and mountains to climb to be together. We also knew that not everyone was as excited as we were. That's okay; we kept believing and pressing on.

God's plan is bigger than any obstacles that try to stand in the way. God is in control. The more you believe and exercise your faith, the more mountains begin to move. The plan starts to unfold and curves right out in front of you.

Others who have ventured down the same path are looking out for you, letting you know that it isn't going to be easy. When you are young in love, nothing else seems to matter. As long as we were together, we could face what we needed to face together. Choosing not to listen to all the negative attitudes that were going on around us was going to be hard. But all of our lives, we would have obstacles to face. The attitude you take toward those obstacles makes a whole world of difference in whether the outcome is good or bad.

You are about to walk out of your familiar box. You think you know it all and you think the world will be the same. It is like living in a fairyland. You meet your Prince Charming and you roll off into the sunset and live happily ever after. When you are young, that is what you think your life will be—just like a fairy tale.

Your expectations are too high. You are living in a dream world. You really want to get into the game of life. You decide to take that leap of faith. When you take that leap, the sky's the limit. Remember, when you fall down, keep getting up. You know that you made the right choice because, after the excitement is all gone, you are still standing and still there, with each other.

Tomorrow always comes, bringing a new and exciting day to begin again. Laughter overpowers the tears throughout the years. The smile remains to take us to another tomorrow. Keep on believing, and each day gets brighter and lighter through all the sorrows. Even when it feels like it is only dark and you are all alone, God hears you talking as your tears hit the floor and your heart breaks. His heart breaks just as yours does and he is with you.

Each day is a new day and begins to heal how you feel, as you learn to pick up the pieces and go on. Each day a new day, it is brighter than before. You dream while you are sleeping, but when your eyes are wide open, you know it is not a dream. It has come true—indeed it has. God's timing is the right timing.

Each morning going to school, I would leave really early to stop by George's house before the start of class. There were times I would not make it to school at all. That year, it seemed, I was out more than I was in. You know eventually you will be caught, but we didn't seem to care. We knew we were destined to be together.

How is it that when you are young, you want to hurry things up? You want to jump with both feet into the journey of life and hang on with both hands. The time had come for the lessons you learn when you know everything there is to know. The things you thought you knew, you did not know at all.

Your parents *do* know what they are talking about, because they lived it. They are there for a reason, but when you're a kid, you do not see the reason. That's okay; the only way to learn is to step out and try it out, have fun along the way, and laugh at the things you learned the hard way.

The day arrived when I got caught at George's house by my mother. Caught with both hands in the cookie jar . . . that feeling you get when you know you're in trouble and the hurt that follows was caused by the choices you made in the moment. When you know you were wrong, you have consequences to face from the choices you made. This was one of those moments in time. When my mother came to the door and words were spoken, I knew what was going to happen before it happened. You can feel the vibe inside.

There was a puzzled look on my mother's face as I got in the truck, and nothing was said on the way home. However, I knew the punishment was coming for the choice I had made. When we arrived home, it was time to face the music, and there was plenty of that. However, that day new choices were given to me. It was up to me to make a choice that day. The choices were to quit school and get a job or quit school and move out. The choice I made was to move out. It has been an adventure every step of the way.

You learn to live by faith more and more each day. You find out real quick that being on your own is a lot different. When you have no plan, you lean on hope and guidance from up above. God is there, even in the middle of the night. In the dark and quiet, you think you're alone, but you're not. He has been with you every step of the way.

Real life is like a fairy tale turned inside out. When you put expectations on others, they always fall short. When you put expectations on God, he always comes through for you; beyond what you could ever imagine it to be.

The way you look at life makes a world of difference. You can give up, or you can get up and press on. Everyone starts the same way at ground zero, and you can soar from zero to hero by not staying down. Get up every time you fall down; you learn something each time. You learn as you go that life is an adventure—sometimes easy and sometimes hard. Jump in and hang on. You will always be surprised, never knowing what's up over the bend of the road.

Keep the faith; it's much better being surprised than knowing what is coming. I have learned so much not knowing than I ever did knowing first. I wouldn't change a thing. It made me who I am today. I am still learning and growing from not knowing. The faith you operate in, you will see in due time. When it is due time, God's time, you will know.

That day I moved out and moved in with George, and the adventure of lifetime began. Make up your mind and don't give up, even when it gets hard. Take a stand. Every step you take is not as hard as it seemed it would be. You learn from each step you take; these are the stepping-stones of life. The choice is yours to stand still or keep walking and learning as you go along.

Enjoy your journey while you can. Remember, everyone stumbles and falls sometimes. Getting up when you fall—that is all that matters. Keep on walking to where you are going. To get to the other side of the mountain is all that matters.

God gives you new mountains to climb and people to meet. Learn to trust him with everything. God sometimes has you out in deep waters where you feel like you are going to drown, but he always throws his line out to you. As you grab onto his line, he always pulls you to safety.

CHAPTER 3

Getting Settled

George and I were settling in together in his trailer house. It was scary and fun all at the same time. In the meantime, George's company laid him off. He had not yet received his first unemployment check.

Shortly after I moved out, my mother came and took my car back, since my car insurance was still under her name. She wouldn't give the car back until we got our own insurance, and that made it real tough finding a job. We had no money and nothing else either. I didn't think a thing about it . . . until I was hungry. The only food in our place was Cheerios and milk, shared with a lot of love. I did not mind as long as we were together.

When George's parents found out that I had moved in, at first they were not too happy about it. It had only been a year or so since his divorce, and they thought he was jumping too quickly into a serious relationship. However, I wanted to let them know that I was different. I loved their son, and I was in it for the long haul, not to just move in and break his heart. After a while, his parents would come by and bring food care packages and help us until George got back on his feet.

Just around the corner was Halloween, our first holiday together in his house. We didn't have a lot of money to spend on candy to hand out. Nevertheless, we knew we needed to get some. So off to the store in town we went and got some caramel treats. It was a lot of fun to see all the costumes the kids were wearing. We gave the whole bag out that night. Thanksgiving was quiet that year; I am not sure what we did. It seemed to fade right into Christmas memories.

I do remember that Christmas like it was yesterday. Early that month, we found out that we were having an addition to our family. Indeed, it took us both by surprise that we were already five months along. By that time, my parents and I were on speaking terms. We finally got the car back after we got our own insurance. After my mom picked me up from my orthodontist appointment—I still had my braces on, not ready to take them off yet—I sprung it on my mom about being a grandma again. I think at the time, she was a little surprised but happy at the same time. At that point, I could not tell for sure what she thought.

Once the shock wore off, she brought over baby clothes from her cedar chest to give us. When I got the baby clothes, we set them on the table in the kitchen. George's parents had stopped by for a little while, but they never noticed the baby clothes on the table.

Our first Christmas together, we went to George's sister Connie's house on Christmas Day, and Christmas Eve we spent at my parent's house. When we were at Connie's, we took her aside to let her know the news of what was coming soon. We asked her not to say anything to the folks yet; we hadn't told them. She was the first one to hear the news on his side. She was just beside herself with joy and happiness for us. She could hardly contain herself. We had a great time at both places.

We thought that we needed to let his folks in on the news too. Therefore, we went out to their house to tell them about our new arrival coming in the spring. They were shocked at first, but once the shock wore off, they told us that we needed to get married right away before the baby was born. George's mom called my mom and arranged a powwow, to talk over what we should do. It was like we had no say in the matter.

It didn't seem like it at the time, but now looking back it was quite comical. At that time, I did not care how it happened, as long as we got married. We decided to go to the justice of the peace to get hitched, and that is exactly what we did on January 27, 1982. We were married and had no clue what lay ahead of us both. All we knew for sure was we were husband and wife with a baby on the way.

By the time we got married, George was back to work at the company that had laid him off. However, I wasn't able to be on his insurance for the pregnancy. Connie found out about this special program down in Denver that we could qualify for. The only catch was that we would have to have the baby in Denver. We were so grateful that Connie hooked us up with that program.

We had no clue what was ahead of us, but we were soon to find out the closer we got to the due date. The date came and went; the baby was on his time, not ours. I went down for my weekly checkup and everything checked out okay. The doctor said, "We will see you this weekend."

Sure enough, Friday evening rolled around and the pain started—slowly at first. I thought it was gas or cramps, Wrong! It was the start of early labor. Who knew? I did not have a clue.

The plan was that we would call George's folks when it was time to go to Denver. Well, that Saturday, it was time to go, as the contractions were getting more intense. Off to Denver we went, making a pit stop by my parents' house first to let them know what was going on.

I was in shock; the words wouldn't come out of my mouth when we got to the hospital, so George spoke up and said, "She's in labor." The whole time coming down to the hospital, everyone was asking, "Are you doing okay?" I was sitting on a blanket just in case my water broke, but it hadn't. Shortly after arriving at the hospital, I got checked in and checked out to see how far along I was. Not quite ready.

The doctor suggested walking around for an hour or so. So that's what we did. We walked and walked until I couldn't walk anymore. Then we went back in my room and the doctor checked me again. I was dilated to an eight. At that time, the doctor decided to break my water to help the labor along.

A little bit later, the baby's heartbeat slowed way down. That's when they rushed me into the delivery room, because the baby needed to come out right away. It was quite frightening. The pain really got intense at that point when it was time to push, especially when they brought out the forceps to straighten the baby. He was trying to come out neck and shoulder first—not good. During the delivery, there were several doctors around watching the baby being born.

We had not realized this was a teaching hospital. Well, doctors have to learn sometime, first by watching and doing as they are learning. The main doctor who was in charge of my delivery room yelled, "Push like a son of gun!" to get the baby here.

"Congratulations, it's a boy," said the doctor. Luke William Hummel was born Saturday May 8, 1982, weighing seven pounds fifteen ounces and measuring twenty-one inches long, at 6:10 p.m.

George and I were so excited about our little bundle of joy. We got Luke's name right out of the Bible. Luke was born the day before Mother's Day. What an awesome gift to receive on such a special day! It was so cute what the nurses did for all the new moms in the nursery. There were gifts in all the baby beds for the moms from the babies. The gifts were a pink carnation and a little note that said how much they loved their mommies.

I knew in my heart that God had blessed us with a real special angel from above, and that was even truer than I knew at the time. Luke and I stayed in the hospital for four days before we were released to go home.

George and I were so nervous to go home with the new baby. We had no clue what was in store for us. We were about to find out the "learn as you go method," like the way everyone else starts out. You think you have it all figured out how your life is going to be. Once a baby comes along, it changes the whole picture of your life.

When you think about it, you have no idea how to take care of a baby, let alone one of your own. Once the baby is here, your instincts kick in. You learn as you go. There is no owner's manual given when you leave the hospital. It's not like buying a car with a warrantee and an instruction book.

In real life, the only owner's manual you will ever need is the Bible. Lots of prayer and talking to God each moment of the day will get you through. It takes a lot of teamwork, and that is part of God's plan, so that we need him each and every day. At times it was a little scary. We tried this and we tried that. We learned as we went along; in other words, we grew up together.

At home with the baby several days later, I found myself overwhelmed, crying a lot, and being moody with the baby. I didn't know it at the time, but I had postpartum depression. I ended up overly tired and mad at the world, and I was taking it out on the baby and yelling and screaming about things, not realizing it was me. It wasn't the baby's fault. Things were not working out as I thought they needed to be.

I thought maybe it was going to take some adjustments that I just needed some rest, and I shook it off. I told myself that things were different now, get used to it. If I would have said to someone how I felt, they would have told me, "You're a mother now, it is your responsibility to take care of the baby." It was my job now.

Thinking back, it's scary what could have happened and didn't. Praise God nothing happened. Thank God he was with me and guided me in what to do; reminding me it would be okay. Keep trusting him, and this too shall pass.

At that time and for years after, I told myself I needed to focus on being a mom right now, so I had to put all my feelings to one side, and that's exactly what I did.

I had made some poor choices in my life, allowing people I thought were my friends to take advantage of me. I was so naive about what was going on, and I did nothing about it. I handled it the wrong way. I pushed my feelings down. I needed to deal with them right then and there. I thought I would deal with it later, but "later" never came; only years went by. And then it was too late—I had already lost myself. I felt like a little girl with no way out but through. God always has a plan, even when you don't have one.

When you find yourself through losing someone, you're self-healing through the brokenness we suffer. Because God loves us, it's not to punish us but to help us to see what is going on. Those were not friends at all; they were hard lessons learned. The best thing to do is to bless and release them and move on.

It has been really hard for me to not stuff my feelings when someone hurts me. I would think it was my fault, I deserved to be hurt. It has been a very hard habit to break—dealing with my feelings *later*. You want to forget each and every time. You keep telling yourself *I will be okay* and acting like nothing ever happened.

You know, tomorrow always comes. You are always forced to deal with things you have been putting off for so long. Someday always comes when you least expect it. The lessons learned you need to face head-on; it's not good for you to stuff your stuff. Face it, release it, learn from it, and move on from it. This is a lesson I've been learning firsthand. As you do, you grow through each and through everything that you face.

That summer after I had Luke, my mom offered to watch him so I could go back to high school and finish. We thought it was a good idea for me to get my diploma. I am really thankful that God showed me what it would be like returning to high school after having Luke. He showed me the true facts of how people treat you when you step out and do something different from everyone else.

My first day back was my last day. I had such high expectations about what it would be like returning. But in the classroom, the teachers and students treated me different from how I thought they would. At lunchtime, I went to sit down at a table of girls who I thought were my friends. Wrong. As I proceeded to sit down, they all got up. Only one remained at the table. The rest went and sat at a different table. It was like I had the plague or something.

The girl who stayed at the table didn't judge me; she accepted me. I know in my heart, God has blessed her in so many ways in her life. It was the love of Jesus that showed me what I needed to see firsthand— the good and the bad. Some people will be nice and some will not be. I learned going back to school was more my plan than God's plan.

God showed me he had a different plan for my life. Like the Bible says, dust your feet off and never return if anyone comes against you and that is exactly what I did. After I ate my lunch, I left and never returned— with any regrets of the decision. I know I've learned more being a mom than I ever did sitting in any classroom.

The whole time I thought I was in control, I was actually following the divine plan that God had laid out for me, without even realizing that I was. He showed me that I had my trust and my expectations in the wrong place. Who cares what others think? I needed to trust God and step out of the boat and aim my expectations in the right direction.

Listen to your heart. God has never steered you wrong in the past; why would he start now? When I started to veer off-course, God redirected me to be exactly where I was needed most: home with Luke, taking care of our little angel. That's where God wanted me to be. Even though I didn't have any idea what I was doing, I listened to my heart and went for it with both eyes wide open.

I took one step at a time, and each day was an adventure. We made it through some way and somehow. God only knows how his plan will come together. We meet in the middle to get where we all need to be— from all the directions and all the paths we take to get to where we need to come together. Each step you take and every decision you make is how your destiny is played out. Life is an adventure, and each day is something that we need to learn from. There is a reason behind each experience we go through. Stop trying to figure out why.

We all are on journeys of our own. Enjoy the moments you have with the ones who are close to you, right where you are. You never know when it will be time for them to fly away. Speak what's in your heart, don't leave words unspoken. You will never leave another day in regret.

Throughout my journey writing and looking back over Luke's life, I see that we all make mistakes; no one's perfect. The mistakes we make, we learn and grow from, each and every one of them. No need to pretend or try to be perfect, because it isn't going to happening. That's not living at all.

You have no need to prove anything to anybody. God knows who we are and what we do, and he loves us just the way we are. So stop being so hard on yourself, by putting unreal expectations on yourself to be perfect.

You need to forgive yourself for all your past mistakes. God has forgiven you, so you need to do the same. He wants to see the real you, the one who makes mistakes and can admit them and learn from them. Learning to forgive your self is the first step of healing. Before you are able to forgive others, you need to forgive yourself. It helps more than you think.

You only hurt yourself when you don't forgive. You try to make everyone else pay for something they had no part of. The best thing to do for yourself is to forgive and move on. Until you do, you'll be stuck in that moment in time. Life is too short to hang on to something that is petty and dumb for no reason at all.

When you hang on to those feelings, the darker you become. When you let them go, the brighter you become. It will be hard at first, but the more you let things go, the easier it becomes. Those are the things that have been holding you back from moving forward. The only way to be free is to name it, face it, forgive it, release it, and move on. When you do, you will see a new light begin to shine in your heart.

Luke had a lot of light shining through him from the way he lived and showed his love for others. He wasn't afraid to tell you or to show you what was in his heart.

Luke was an easygoing baby. He loved to eat and wasn't afraid to try things. When Luke was able to eat big people's food, his favorites were bologna and bananas—not together, of course. When he got older, it was pizza and burgers and fries. He was not much of a sweet eater, more of a meat-and-potatoes guy. He would let you know right away what he didn't like, such as lobster and things that looked to foreign to him. He didn't want any part of that. Otherwise, he would try a new recipe now and then.

Luke was three months old when we decided to take him to get his picture taken at Kmart. He was propped up there as he was getting his first picture taken by a photographer. He wasn't quite ready to smile a fully elated smile, but his baby grin was so cute with his big blue eyes. It was so hard to choose which pictures we wanted to keep. When we got home, we started sending pictures to family and friends. Everyone loved them.

Around the same time, one of the Denver stations, during the morning broadcast, mentioned that you could send your baby's picture in and they would show it on the program. So we decided to send Luke's picture in, and it was so exciting to see his picture on the program. We even had friends and family call about the picture on the show. He was a young celebrity.

We spent Luke's first Thanksgiving at George's parents' house. The whole family was there, and it was a lot of fun. Christmas of 1982 was another day to remember. We had a huge snowstorm that closed the whole state for a few days. It started snowing early Christmas Eve morning and snowed pretty much throughout the day. The snow got so heavy that the lines began to fall off the power poles on the east side of town where we lived. So off to my mother's house we drove; she had a fireplace and power.

It was quite an adventure getting there in the Chevy Vega we were driving at the time. It was getting real late by the time we got to Grandma's safe and sound. It was time to lay Luke down for the night shortly after we arrived. We didn't have a baby bed for him, so we made do with what we had. My mom got out one of her dresser drawers, which she turned into a bed for the night. It was so cute seeing Luke sleeping soundly in the drawer. We even took pictures to show him when he grew up where he slept during the snowstorm.

The next day, the storm had lifted. It was time for the big dig-out and the adventure back home when the time was right and the power was restored.

Soon it was Luke's first birthday, and it was party time. We had it at George's parents, Grandma J. and Papa Frank's house .The cake was a football-field cake with the uprights and all. It was so cute. As he dove into the cake, Luke smiled from ear to ear, wearing cake head to toe. It was a day we will never forget. Just thinking about it brings a smile to my face and joy to my heart.

As time went by, Luke began to crawl and to sit up. Sitting up was a struggle; it seemed like he was off-balance a little bit in the beginning. It was more comfortable for him once he learned his own balance. Then he was okay with it.

Every day brought a new surprise as Luke grew into a little boy. After reaching a year old, he still wasn't walking yet and that concerned us. So we contacted a doctor to have Luke checked out to see if something was wrong. I knew in my heart there was.

The doctor said Luke was okay and not to worry about it. He would walk when he was ready. As the days and weeks went by, though, Luke still wasn't walking yet. George and I thought we would teach him to walk. We tried everything and nothing worked.

George's mom came by to take Luke for a visit and said, "I can teach Luke to walk." George and I thought, *Yeah, right.* But maybe he just needed a grandma's touch. When she brought him back to us Sunday night, he was walking. We were so amazed and grateful.

It was God showing us a miracle right in front of our eyes. What a blessing! It was great to see Luke walking across the floor. *Thank you, Lord, for the love you have shared with us, through Luke, the special gift you gave us.*

Next, it was time to potty-train. Now that's a story in itself. We tried everything to get Luke to go potty in the pot. It just wasn't happening. It was under Luke's timing, not ours. He did eventually get the concept. But if he was busy playing outside, he would forget and would have an accident or two. After days of pulling my hair out, I finally told him, "I don't care if you are outside playing, you still need to go to the bathroom. Even if you have to go behind a tree or a bush, when you need to go, just go."

To my surprise, he listened and did just that—in front of the next-door neighbor's trailer house. Of course, one of the neighbors saw and told us about it. Well, it's better than doing it in his pants, as I said at the time.

Who cares? He wasn't hurting anyone. The neighbor next door didn't care, he actually laughed about it. Looking back, everyone gets so worked up over all the little things. That includes me as well, as I struggled to learn to let things go of all the little petty things that used to bother me so. They're not worth all that fuss.

It's a waste of time to worry about things we have no control over. Let go and go on. Needless to say, Luke got potty-trained, and the neighbor's flowers were brighter than ever.

Luke's first Halloween party was at his Aunt Jan's house. The costume he wore was a navy sailor. Luke was so cute, we took pictures. He wasn't too happy about getting them taken before the party. He wanted down so he could go play. We got to the party, and all the other kids were dressed up as well. During the party, they played games and received lots of candy. Luke had so much fun, when we got home and his head hit the pillow he was fast asleep.

Luke enjoyed most holidays, including the Fourth of July. He loved the colors of the fireworks in the sky. Luke lit a few sparklers after dark. Luke's favorite holiday was Christmas, and celebrating Jesus' birthday made it even more special. Luke's face would light up each and every time he saw Santa. Luke believed in Jesus and Santa every day of his life. Luke's faith was so strong you could see it in his eyes. The strength he got from our heavenly father showed each and every day.

CHAPTER 4

New Addition

Before we knew it, there was another one on the way. That summer was not so bad at all, and those nine months went by quick. I knew Luke was going to my mom's in Nebraska where she moved to this summer, the week before the baby was due. Luke was so excited because he got to ride in Grandpa's eighteen wheeler with the trailer attached all the way to Grandma's house. Off they went. Luke was three at the time; it seemed like yesterday he was born.

That Monday, I had an appointment with the doctor for my weekly checkup. The doctor told me that it wouldn't be long now. Pretty much the rest of the week, I cleaned and cleaned to get ready for the new arrival.

Friday morning, I woke up with a bloody nose. I called the doctor in a panic, and he said that it was normal. We finally got it under control. Then, shortly after George left to go to work, my pains started. *Here we go.* I called the doctor again; he wanted me to come in about two o'clock that afternoon to be checked. In the meantime, he suggested that I walk and walk; it would help with my contractions. So I put a phone call in to George and let him know what was going on. That is all it took—he was at the house in a flash. That day, I think his car had angel wings attached to it.

We went for a walk around the trailer court several times until it was time to go to the doctor's office. We decided to put the hospital bag in the backseat just in case we were hospital-bound. We arrived at the office shortly before two o'clock and the door was locked. We began to wait for the office to open, thinking maybe a late lunch—not realizing it was Friday and the office closed at noon on Friday. When I talked to the office earlier that morning, nothing was mentioned about closing at noon. My mind wasn't on what day it was; it was on the labor pains.

After waiting for a while in front of the office, I felt my contractions getting closer. That's when we headed over to the hospital, where we were admitted and then hooked up to all the machines. Now it was a waiting game for the doctor's arrival.

First the doctor on call needed to be located to let him what was going on. It has been a joke ever since that he was out playing golf. When the doctor arrived, he asked if I would like to speed up the process a little. I said yes, and he broke my water. He said he would be back in a few hours to deliver the baby. Sure enough, the show got on the road within a few hours. The real hard labor was in full force, and then it was time to push like crazy.

The baby's head began to crown before the doctor could get his hands completely washed and dry. The nurse and George said to hurry up before the baby landed on the floor. You know how it goes—right time, right place.

The doctor yelled out, "Congratulations, it's a girl." Our precious baby girl was born on October 18, 1985. The day of her arrival, her father blessed her with the beautiful name of Latisha Marie. Soon as she arrived, we called Luke to let him know he was a big brother. He was so excited to get home and meet his little sister.

In the beginning, Luke was a big help—until the new wore off. Then he wanted to know when she was going home. Once we explained to him this *was* her home, he was okay with it. Luke gave his sister a nickname of Tic. It was cute on the day when Luke got in trouble for something; his first response was Tic did it . . . while she was fast asleep in her bassinette.

Shortly after having Latisha I went to work as a cashier. George was laid off, and jobs were really hard to find and to keep, because they would hire for a while and then let you go. In the early '80s, it seemed like you did what you had to do, and you trusted everything would work out, and it always did one way or another.

I worked for six months, and by then George had landed a good job as a trash man for a local company. His boss was nice, and we got to ride with George from time to time on his route. We got to see all the odd things people would throw out, such as grass clippings and dog poop. But rarely would we see any household trash at some of the stops. It was odd; what were they eating, or did they eat out all the time? It makes you wonder.

We gave up on trying to figure out why people do the things they do. George did find some awesome treasures in the trash that we used in our garage sale. Some we kept for ourselves. We had a fun day selling and meeting lots of people.

The kids really enjoyed going with daddy in his truck on the holidays, because on occasion the kids would get treats from the ladies on the route.

At first, while George and I were both working, we were blessed with a wonderful sitter for the kids. Then shortly after the holidays, she informed us that she was moving and could no longer watch them. A friend referred us to someone else she knew. After meeting and visiting with this woman, we thought she was a good choice. After three day, *wrong!* We never returned. We decided that for me to stay home and take care of the kids would be the best choice of all.

CHAPTER 5

A Storm Comes

April 3, 1986, while we still lived in the trailer court, there was a big snowstorm. During the storm, the snow got so deep; George was unable to drive home in the car after his route. So he ended up driving the trash truck home so he would be able to do his route in the morning.

George made it home no problem, but parking the truck in the front of the house was a different story. There was a lot of ice built up on the mirrors, and with the roads being slick; it was difficult to back up. He wound up sliding into the trailer and knocking it off its perch. We were all inside while this went on. Luke was riding his little car inside the trailer, and he was launched off of it. The baby slept through the whole thing. We all ended up going to stay with friends because we had no power or heat.

The day after the storm, we went back to the trailer, and by then the power and the heat were back on. George looked at the trailer a little closer, and after further review, it was just bumped a little off of the perch. He decided it was okay for us to be there, and then George went on his way to finish his route.

The snow was still too deep to bring the car back home, so he came home in the trash truck once again and parked out front. That didn't set well with our trailer guard of the park that evening, so he posted a note on our door about the truck—that we needed to move it or else.

So where could we move it with all the snow? We didn't move the truck, and as a result, we were evicted. Looking back, the snowstorm was a blessing. We needed to get started with a new chapter of the journey. We would look for a new place to live.

We had an appointment down in Denver at the university to see what was going on with Luke—why he wasn't talking and why he was getting around very slowly. Luke was three years old at the time and Latisha was six months. While we were down there, the doctors gave Luke a complete once-over. They were really concerned about Luke's calves being a bit larger than normal. The doctors wanted our whole family history, especially when we told them about my uncles who had muscular dystrophy. That sent up a red flag, but the only way to know for sure was a muscle biopsy on one of Luke's calves.

We made Luke's biopsy appointment for the following week. The day arrived, and he was just getting over an ear infection. The doctors gave us something to relax Luke, or in other words, to slow him down. Instead, it charged his battery, and he was running all over the place.

When the nurse called us back into the room, she couldn't believe her eyes. The drug was supposed to relax him, not make him more active. When it finally took hold, the doctors numbed the area they need for the biopsy of the leg. We didn't know what to expect until we were in the middle of the biopsy. Luke couldn't feel anything, but it was quite frightening for him. While the procedure was going on, Luke began screaming and squirming and wanted to get away. We ended up holding him down so he wouldn't move.

I was upset, and I told the doctors never again unless he was put to sleep. I learned so much that day—to ask questions about everything no matter what was going on. Later on that week, we got the results back from the biopsy, and they confirmed that Luke had Duchene muscular dystrophy. The doctors explained all about the form that Luke had, what kind of life he would have, what he would endure in the stages he would go through from the beginning to the end, and his life expectancy—late teens or early twenties.

Duchene muscular dystrophy is genetically passed down to the son from the mother, who carries the bad gene. The gene can be passed to daughters who then pass it on to their sons when they have kids. But it depends on how the gene falls for that to happen. In other words, some will and some won't be carriers of the bad gene.

Our whole family got tested, and a few were carriers and some were not. Luke's sister was also tested; she was six months old at the time. The doctors said that she was a carrier of the gene, but that since she was so young, we should have her tested again later on when she was old enough to have kids of her own. With all the new testing coming out, by then more advanced testing would be available.

When we heard what they were telling us, it was hard to fathom. Luke was three years old, looking happy and having fun, and suddenly we were hearing that he would only be with us for a short time. Our minds were racing. It was overwhelming to take in so much information all at once. The doctors did say to treat Luke like one of the other kids, not to set him up on a shelf like a china doll, afraid that he was going to break.

While we were in Denver, we met with the genetic doctors and provided further information on our family history. The rest of the girls (cousins) were tested to see if they were also carriers.

The doctors also wanted us to do some developmental testing to see where he was at. After all the testing at the center, they said that Luke needed to start in a special-education program. The program that he would attend was Foot Hills Gateway, which was located in Fort Collins; Colorado. This was before the special-education program was first introduced to the regular school system. Introducing it to the school system was a good idea, because it would allow all the kids to experience everything that life is all about. All kids get to learn and grow from one another.

From that day forward, we didn't focus on how long we had with Luke. We focused on the here and now, the journey that God had laid out for us. I'm so glad we were able to live one day at a time, not knowing what was coming next. If you knew everything ahead of time, you would never grow into the person God wants you to be.

Each day is a stepping-stone in life. What you do with the stones each day is the test you take. Some tests are hard and some are easy. It's the way you view them that determines how many times you get to take them. It is up to you to make the choice.

I took it upon myself to be perfect in everything. Then there would be no question about whether it was right or wrong—it would be perfect. I would have a fit when things weren't perfectly done right. Looking back,

I know it was a stepping-stone, and things didn't need to be perfect to be right. Forgive yourself and others. No one is perfect. Let it go and move on.

It takes many years to find this out. We need each other, and we are on the same journey together. We all need to get along with each other. We all make mistakes; they make us who we are. Being perfect is being so unrealistic in your thinking. Change your way of thinking and change the way you are living.

CHAPTER 6

The Big Move

Our search was over: we located a little house in Loveland. We all were excited about the move and we gathered up boxes and started to pack. Luke was really excited because he was starting school. He went three days a week and three hours a day to start out for the first year.

The week we started moving, while George and Luke were at school and at work, Latisha and I would bring over little things that would fit in the car. By the time George got off work, he could start moving over the bigger items. When the weekend rolled around, we had most of it done, so the move wouldn't take so long.

The last thing we brought to the new house was a puppy George had received from his boss. The puppy was so cute. Her name was Sass. Luke had a ball with her; they had so much fun together.

We have lots of stories about Luke and that puppy. One time, while the puppy was sleeping on Luke's favorite blanket, Luke grabbed hold of the blanket and pulled the puppy all around the yard. It was so cute that the puppy slept the whole time. Another story is that George was teaching the puppy tricks with treats. One of the tricks in particular that I recall was how the puppy would sit up and beg. Luke saw that, and that's all it took for him to try it out on his sister. We saw him as we came around the corner. He had a piece of cheese dangling over her head trying to get her to beg, saying, "Pretty Tic, pretty Tic." We laughed and laughed over that.

Once we got all settled in, George and I planned a birthday party for Luke in our new house. We invited the whole family for a barbeque, cake, and ice cream. Prior to Luke's party, his aunt Connie sent him some balloons for his birthday. Luke was so excited about the balloons when they arrived. He wanted to take the balloons outside, and not knowing what could happen, he proceeds outdoors with them. Before I could say, "Don't let go," it happened. The balloons were heading up toward the sky in that moment.

Luke wanted me to climb up the tree to get them down for him. I really felt bad for him; they were gone in a flash. It was a hard lesson learned, and from that day he would hold onto them tight. Everyone came to his party; it was so much fun. Grandpa brought his big truck for Luke and all the others kids too, to give them all rides. That made the day complete.

You don't know why things are short-lived or why things change, but they do. A month later, our landlord contacted us to let us know the rent was going up starting next month. This actually happened to the previous tenants too. The rent was real reasonable at first, and then they jacked it up after you were in.

Our house in Loveland was short-lived, but that's okay—it was part of God's plan. He always has his reasons. We moved back to Berthoud in the apartments where my brother and his wife lived at the time. In fact, we were right next door. Living next door to each other, my brother and I got closer—in fact, we all did. It was a short time later that my brother and his wife divorced. He needed us as much as we needed him. We all had a lot of fun living by each other.

Luke was now riding the bus to Ft. Collins to school. Luke got ready for school with his little backpack—so grown up. He was always excited about going to school and learning so much. It had a lot to do with his teacher; she had a special knack for teaching and spurred his willingness to learn.

The first time we meet Dee Ann, we knew there was something special about her. I now know that God sent Dee Ann to us to be Luke's teacher. She was Luke's guardian angel to teach him and to be with him at school. Most of all, he trusted her. It was awesome how she taught those kids.

When Luke first started school, he didn't talk very much. Soon things began to change, and it was like night and day. Luke was in Dee Ann's class for a year and half, and he spent other half in Head Start.

Before going on to kindergarten, the kids had a graduation ceremony. It was so cute. As they walked across the stage to get their diplomas, they all looked so grown up.

You know how fast summer comes and goes. Another school year was upon us. This year was going to be a little different, not having Dee Ann around. In the morning, Luke would go to Loveland for kindergarten and the Gain (special learning) program. Berthoud hadn't yet started the Gain program in its schools. Then, in the afternoon, he would go to the Berthoud kindergarten. His Berthoud teacher's name was Ms. Leonard; later that year she was married, and then she became Mrs. Mirch.

Luke talked a lot about the things he learned. Some of the things he enjoyed and some he didn't, but he was always willing to give it a try. The school in Berthoud was talking about bringing the Gain program there. It needed to, because the following year the kids from Foot Hills Gateway would be going to school there as well as Loveland.

The school was interviewing two people for the job, and one of them was Dee Ann Wilson. When we saw the principal in the hall, she asked what our thoughts were, since Luke would be one of the students in the class. We made a suggestion about Dee Ann Wilson and how much she helped Luke while she was his teacher.

We felt so blessed that the principal valued our opinion. We knew this was part of God's plan. Dee Ann started that fall at Berthoud Elementary and has been there ever since. Every child she has taught loves her and has learned so much. Every day, Luke would come home with a smile on his face and a story to share about what he had learned that day.

It was time to move again. We found a duplex with a garage that had become available. For the first time, the kids would have their own rooms. Yes! So we moved in. This was the first time Luke got to go to camp. I don't who was more scared, Luke or I. Once Luke arrived at camp, I called to see if he made it okay. The camp director told me not to worry, Luke was in good hands. Each camper had his own helper who was assigned for the week.

The whole week was planned around what Luke wanted to do. On Wednesday, we went up to visit Luke at camp and have lunch with him. The day we went up, there was a show that was put on. It was so cute. The kids really enjoyed it as well as the adults. Throughout the week, Luke enjoyed fishing, horseback riding, riding on a Harley, swimming in the warm pool, and all sorts of other fun activates. When he got home, he talked for days about all the fun he had. Luke couldn't wait until next year so he could go again.

CHAPTER 7

The Trip and Purchase of Our Own Home

Later on that summer, after Luke got back from camp, Latisha and I were invited to go on a trip with my mom and dad and a few other family members. The trip was to New Mexico to see my brother and his family and then to Las Vegas to see my sister and her family as well. Along the way, we would see the Grand Canyon and the Hoover Dam. It sounded like a great time, and we had all the details all worked out.

During that time George and Luke were going to have some boy time together. The day we left, Luke would stay the night at George's parent's house. Luke loved staying at Grandma's and Papa's. He could play until George got off of work and then George would pick him up.

It was okay for about a day, but Luke kept asking where we were. He knew we were leaving and was okay with everything until it came right down to it. The more he realized we were not coming home for a while, the more he thought we weren't coming home al all. We talked on the phone, but it didn't matter to him.

While we were gone, Luke developed a rash all over his little body. George had to take Luke to the doctor to see what it was. He found out the rash was worry bumps, so the doctor gave him some ointment to put on them. It was harder on Luke being away from his mom and sister than we really thought it would be. Soon as Latisha and I arrived home, the bumps disappeared. From that day forward, it was hard for me to go somewhere and leave Luke at home. We had a special trust bond with each other.

The summer was coming to an end, and another school year was upon us. This year was more exciting than ever, because Dee Ann Wilson was back in Luke's life once again. Our prayers were answered; we were so grateful and thankful. This year, Latisha got to go to Head Start, and she was so excited to be going to school like her big brother.

We were able to get our own house—the perfect house, just the right size for us. We were so blessed, because it was exactly what we had been dreaming of. In the mixed of the big move, we were so proud of George taking a leap of faith and starting HVAC classes. While he was doing that at night, I was taking care of the kids and also taking a home course in interior design. It was so much fun.

Prior to doing this home course, I received my GED. I wanted to set a good example that you can do anything if you set your mind to it and am willing to do what it takes. In other words, you do your part and God will do his part.

In my heart, I also wanted to do hair and nails as well. I felt deep inside that I needed to learn something that I could do from home down the road. So I jumped in with both feet and went for it and achieved the goal that I set out to do. The kids encouraged us every step of the way. There were times that were hard, but the little voices said, "Keep on going, you're almost there. Don't give up now, one more mile, keep pressing on."

In 1989, George graduated HVAC School with perfect attendance and an award. In 1989, I received my GED, finished my interior-design course, and in 1991 graduated cosmetology school. Also, we moved into our new house that we'd dreamed about long ago. The next seven years we lived in the little house in Berthoud and made some great memories there.

The summer of 1991, George's aunt Colleen set the ball rolling to get a special trip through the Make-A-Wish program. Luke got to choose where he wanted to go, and he chose Disneyland in California. We were so blessed; God had arranged everything from start to the finish. We are so thankful and grateful that we got to experience such a wonderful trip.

It was wonderful how it happened, and each moment is a memory we will never forget.

Luke got to go up in front and meet the pilots who were flying the plane. Luke's name was announced over the loudspeaker to let everyone know about the special guest on board, and that also made his flight extra special. When we arrived at the hotel, the board as we walked in had Luke's name on it to welcome him. In our room there were T-shirts, little stuffed animals for both of the kids, and a large fruit basket.

Our stay at the hotel was fun, with swimming and, across the parking lot, a restaurant where the kids got to eat whatever they wanted. Each day there was something new and different on the menu. It didn't matter what we ordered, it was great. Once we got to Disneyland, Luke and Latisha rode on all the rides they could. Just looking at them, you knew in your heart they were in heaven.

Each one of the kids got an autograph book for the characters to sign while they were there. Their smiles grew bigger and brighter each time they saw another character and received a signature. We all felt like kids again. George's parents and my brother and a friend of his came along to enjoy all the fun. It was a real special treat to have others join in the experience.

George's parents videotaped the whole trip. I felt so blessed to have such a special gift. The tapes of memories are for us to enjoy for years to come and to share with others. The kids didn't complain about anything. Their dream had come true.

Grown-ups sometimes should stop and look at childlike faith; life would be a lot simpler for them. Kids believe in love and share it with everyone. Take a closer look at your kids and see what they see. Start living with your heart, believe in love, and share some today. Your heart will fill with joy.

The week slowly came to an end, and it was time to fly back home. We brought a surprise for Colleen to thank her for putting Luke's name in for the Make-A-Wish.

When we got back, the following week it was time for Luke to go to camp. While Luke was gone, we created a surprise of our own for when he got home. The surprise was, we painted and gave his room a makeover.

While Luke was at camp, he caught a trout out of the lake. Thank goodness they already froze the fish before he brought it home! He was so excited to tell us all about how he and his helper caught the fish. The rest of his stay at camp was a lot of fun too. When he told us stories about camp, his eyes would light up and his face would just glow.

That afternoon when he went into his new room, he smiled from ear to ear. He absolutely loved it.

Summer was coming to an end. This year at school, the kids' Grandma J. would be in charge of the lunchroom. She also helped prepare the hot lunches that were served. The kids were so excited that they were able to see Grandma every day for lunch. Then, when it was Grandparent's Day, both grandmas were there to enjoy lunch with the kids. This year, the school decided on Halloween they would do a pumpkin-decorating contest. All the parents helped the kids with their pumpkins. It was a family affair.

After all the pumpkins were brought in, throughout the week they would be voted on. You were to write down and vote on the ones you liked the best. Once that was done, the winners would be announced.

That year, Luke and Latisha's pumpkin got first place. We were so proud of them. We took pictures of the pumpkin and the kids. Each year, the kids dressed up as something different. It made it fun trying to figure what to dress up as.

Going trick-or-treating was fun, even though it was usually freezing. But it didn't matter to the kids; we still ventured out for a little while, until our hands and our faces were about to fall off, and then it was time to venture back home and unthaw and finally go off to bed to get rested for school the next day. The most important thing was all the candy they received and all the fun and smiles and memories they made.

CHAPTER 8

The First Ski Trip to Winter Park

The kids were all back in school after Christmas break. All the students in Luke's Gain class were so excited to go skiing at Winter Park. A list of items was sent home that would be needed to go, such as snow pants and all the warm things you could think of. When Luke went to school the day of the ski trip, he was bundled up from head to toe. I am so surprised he could sit or even get around with all the clothes that he had on. We wanted to make sure he was warm enough, that he wouldn't get cold or catch a cold by being cold.

It was an all-day affair. The kids left home at five in the morning and returned home at six thirty that evening. When Luke arrived home, he was totally exhausted from his all-day activity. Luke got the hang of it skiing; someone went along and steadied him one side as they went down the hill together. The next day we decided to keep Luke home, because his legs were really weak and unsteady. Rest is what he needed most.

When Latisha went to school that day, I told her to let Mrs. Wilson know that Luke wouldn't be at school because he was too tired from yesterday's ski trip. Soon after that conversation, Mrs. Wilson got on the phone with us to see what was going on. Dee Ann recalled Luke falling a couple times but didn't think he broke his leg. We reassured her that he hadn't broken a thing. Latisha had changed up the message a little. We let Dee Ann know the real reason why Luke was staying home for the day. It's funny how little kids' minds work and the stories they can change around.

New renters moved into the house across the street from where we lived. It was a single lady with her kids. All the kids were playing outside together. As I looked outside, the other kids were making fun of Luke and the way he was walking, and that was all it took. It really upset me, and I started saying some unpleasant words to them and sent them home.

Shortly after that, the kids' mother came home. The mother came right over and wanted to know what went on. I asked her what her son had told her, and then I informed her that was not the whole story and finished it for her. I apologized to her and her son for the way the situation was handled. She said no, she would have done the same thing.

A short time later, the kids came over to apologize to Luke. After all that, all the kids in the neighborhood got along great. We never had to worry about the kids being mean to him again in our neighborhood.

All the kids in Luke's class loved him. Luke always thought of everyone but himself. If you got anything new, he would notice. Luke spoke the truth when he gave his opinion about something, good or bad, even if some of his answers weren't what you wanted to hear.

He would compliment you on your outfit and your hairstyle. He would also let you know when you needed a breath mint—not to hurt you by telling you that, but to help. Luke always kept everyone on time. Like when the kids had a class they needed to attend, he would remind them so they wouldn't be late or miss it. He also kept the teachers on track as well. The teachers would tell Luke, "Don't let me forget" whatever they needed to remember.

Luke always knew if you were at school or not. Then, when the student or the adult would return, he would ask, "Were you sick? Are you feeling better?" Luke would always ask how you are today, no matter how he felt that day. Luke always knew what to say to make you feel better. No matter what was going on in his world, he always had a positive word to encourage you, with a smile to seal the deal. At parent-teacher conferences, we always heard positive things about Luke and Latisha.

Luke always spoke highly of his sister, no matter what. Latisha adored her brother and looked up to him. She was a little spitfire from day one, especially when it came to her family or her brother. Latisha holds her own and is not afraid to speak her mind; always fighting for what she thinks is right at the time, never backing down, and standing up for her self and others who can't. She's there when it really counts.

Latisha grew up real fast; she knew in her heart she needed to be strong-willed person. Latisha was one of Luke's guardian angels throughout his life. There would come a day when he would be hers.

There was a day in school on the playground when a student said bad things about Luke. When Latisha heard, she flew down off that slide and started wailing on the boy. It took a teacher to pull her off. Don't think that student ever said anything bad about someone else ever again.

Luke and Latisha had their little brother-and-sister fights like most kids have; it's part of growing up. Most of the time, though, they got along and played together, such as playing Barbie's , and GI Joes when they were little. As they got older, they moved up to Lego's and cars and trucks with the cities. One year for Christmas, Latisha got rollerblades that she used to push Luke in his manual wheelchair around the block and up and down the sidewalk, even to Grandma's house.

On one of the visits out to Grandma's house, their cousin Ryan was up visiting from Denver. The kids were all playing together outside, and the adults were on the porch visiting. We heard the kids playing, and Ryan convinced Luke to touch Papa's hot fence, which was on at the time to keep the cows in. So Luke proceeded to touch the fence, and nothing happened. Ryan then proceeded to touch the fence, and it lit him up. The angels were on the top of things that day, and it backfired on Ryan.

Another day the angels were on duty: While Luke was at his aunt Jan's house playing, a kid who usually ran through the house like a chicken with his head cut off came around the corner and ran right into Luke. It didn't faze Luke at all, but the other kid was screaming his head off. From that day forward, that kid slowed down after that head-on. Luke's angel was on duty that day. Take a look and see how many times your angel is on duty for you without you even knowing it—a lot more than you think.

CHAPTER 9

Curves Ahead

In the spring of 1991, we asked really good friends of ours if they would be the kids' godparents. Both couples agreed. My brother's girls were baptized on the same day as well. After the baptism ceremony, we had a picnic set up. We all had a great time.

Later that summer, Papa's pig was going to have babies, and the kids were so excited to see and touch the piglets. They also got to see calves being born. It was like the kids had their own petting zoo right outside of town. We have pictures of Luke in his little farm outfit with the biggest smile on his face, going down to feed the baby calves. It's so cute. Every time you see the picture, it melts your heart.

Each summer after Luke would get back from camp and before school started up again, all our families would get together for a large picnic. It was a lot of fun seeing all the cousins, making memories you will remember for a lifetime.

What a joyful summer it had been. Then it was time for back-to-school, and soon the holidays were approaching. Halloween was a treat: Luke dressed as a lion and Latisha was a pumpkin. They were so cute. Thanksgiving was a time to be thankful that year more than we knew.

Days go by and things are going fine. You think that everything is going the way it should be, and then . . .

Life is too short, and it's not a game that you can do over. Life is about a lot more than who is right and who is wrong. Life is sometimes made up of hard lessons learned, but when you grow, you become wiser.

Don't take life for granted or the people in it. Life is a gift. Your loved ones are a blessing from God.

You think your loved ones will always be there, but you never know when their time is up. Be quick to forgive, tell everyone you're sorry when you are, tell everyone how you feel now. Don't put it off until tomorrow—tomorrow may be too late. Too often when tomorrow comes, we live in regret of yesterday. So when today comes, God gives us the grace to start again. Listen to your heart. God loves us so much. He wants us to learn from our mistakes and move on from them. That's why he gives us a clean slate each morning of every day.

Enjoy your loved ones each and every day, because you never know when they will be called home. What I've been learning is to be grateful and thankful about everything, not just at Thanksgiving.

Christmas time around our house was exciting—our favorite time of the year. It was so cute seeing all the kids up onstage for the Christmas program, each one singing his or her little heart out for everyone to enjoy. Christmas break was around the corner, and soon the kids would be able to sleep in and enjoy the break and no school. When families get together, some memories you remember, some you soon forget, and some bring smiles to your face. The special times you remember in your heart are your memories that no one can take from you.

Each and every day, life throws a curve your direction that you were not prepared for. You can face it head-on or deal with it later. Change quite a bit or change a little, it is still change, no matter how big or small it is. You feel lost not knowing what to do next; you build up a wall of pain that no one can climb.

We can learn so much from kids, who are not afraid to show pain when they are hurting. They grow as they trust and learn not to fear things that they have no choice but to face. Everyone hurts sometimes. Why does everyone think you have to hurry up and get over what you have been through, with all your pain? You don't allow yourself to grieve the way you need to; you bury it and try to get over it. Who cares what others think about how long it takes to get over losing someone that you loved very much?

Children show us how to be real—how to accept things that can't be changed and be willing to change things we can, how to have an open heart to share what they see and live life bold and admit we they have made mistakes.

My brother was a kid at heart, always living his life to the extreme, never afraid to try something new. He never cared what others thought of his actions—just the way God made him, unique in every way. He was true to himself, followed his heart, did exactly what he wanted to do, and enjoyed ever moment of his journey. Even though his journey was short, he touched everyone in a special way that you could never forget.

He lived life *boldly*, to the fullest, full-bore, until his road ran out of pavement, never looking back in regret, always moving straight ahead, never looking back. He knew that what was behind him was done. Looking straight ahead, there was always something new for him to see and try. For sure, his vision was bigger than we could ever imagine, and that was seeing Jesus face to face.

With the faith of a child, Luke wasn't worried about what happened. He wanted to play hide and seek with his dad in the house for a while. I think it was a way to get his dad's mind off what was going on around them. Luke found a great hiding spot, and it took his dad quite a while to find him. Luke kept calling his dad to come to find him. George looked everywhere in the house; finally, he looked in the clothes dryer, and sure enough, that's exactly where Luke was. I don't know how he got in there, but he did. When his dad opened the door of the dryer, Luke poked his head out and said, "Hi, Dad!"

When you look at things through kids' eyes, you know how to make things better. Even when you think it's too hard, the story always brings a smile to my face. Each and every curve that comes your way seems hard at the time while you are there. But God is preparing you for what lies ahead, and he will be with you every step of the way.

Each stone that is put in place makes you the person you are. Everything happens for a reason, and when you are able to see the bigger picture, you will understand a little more about why. As time goes by, you learn to focus on what really matters, such as the good things that happen more than the unhappy times. You learn from them both that sometimes the darkest hour can also be the closet hour with God. He will show you the light to bring you through.

Keep looking ahead each and every day. You know in your heart that the friends and family who have gone home before you, you'll see again. Picking up the pieces and moving forward when you fall down is when the healing begins, and the light will shine through once again as you pick up the pieces one by one. Slowly the light begins to shine, and in time it is God that you see. He is with you in the good times as well as the bad, with you in the dark and in the light, shining in every delightful smile you see.

CHAPTER 10

Casts On, Casts Off

A snowstorm shut down the town for a few days, with no power and no school. The kids went outside to play in the snow and make a snowman. George helped them; he was like a big kid himself. The snowman was very large—about six feet tall and about four feet around—with a hat, nose, buttons down his belly, sticks for hands (one holding a can of beer), and a scarf around his neck. It was so cute how it all came together.

Luke caught the flu, and it lingered on a lot longer than it should have. The longer it stayed, the worse Luke got. I called the doctor, and she wanted to see him right away. Then the doctor said he needed to be admitted in the hospital.

At the time, George was at work, so I called him to let him know what was going on. He came home and we took Luke to the hospital together. Luke was really dehydrated, so they hooked him up to an IV and filled his tank and flushed him out. He was good as new, back to his cheerful self.

Later that spring, we ventured down to Denver for one of Luke's doctor appointments. The doctor suggested that Luke have surgery to do a tendon release in the back of his ankle so he wouldn't have to walk on his tiptoes to get around. This should help with his balance and his mobility. The surgery went well, but the catch was that Luke would have it be in a cast for a while.

Luke was a trouper the whole time he was in the cast. Then it was time to get the cast off, and his ankle looked great. The doctor said to come back in six months and we would see how it looked then. Luke was getting around pretty good, even though one calf was still smaller than the other. The difference was amazing—you could see it. We all thought if it worked once, it would work again. So we set another surgery date to do the same surgery to the other leg.

The second cast was taken off on a Friday, and Luke seemed more tired on Saturday, so he rested the whole day. Then on Sunday, we got ready to go to the store in Loveland to buy groceries for the week. While we were checking out with the groceries, Luke needed to go to the bathroom before our drive home, so off he went. Throughout the time at the checkout, we kept hearing George's name over the intercom. So George went over to customer service to see what was going on.

Luke had fallen in the bathroom trying to open that heavy door to get out—his legs gave out, and down he went. When his dad got to him, the manager was talking to Luke to see if he was okay and if he needed anything. Luke said, "I will be okay." He just wanted his dad to take him home.

George got him to the car and he seemed to be okay. As the day went on, his leg really started hurting him more and more, and by the end of the day he couldn't put any weight at all on it. It had to be something more than just a sprung foot.

That evening when Luke went to bed, we talked about going to have it checked out. The doctor X-rayed his leg and saw a slight crack, and then he sent us down to Longmont to have a cast put on. Luke was so excited he got to pick out the color of his cast. When the cast was put on, though, he wouldn't able to put any weight on his leg for a few days.

As we were trying to get Luke loaded in the car, we turned it into a fun adventure, and those are the times you remember the most—the times you have no clue how you are going to do something. All you want to do is cry, and all you do is laugh. You find a way through laughter, and it gets done, no problem at all. This was one of those times; both of us began to laugh, and we got him in no problem.

Now it was time to get him in the house, so our idea was to put Luke on my back and give him a piggyback ride. It went pretty well until we started to lift off with the weight of the leg with the cast on it. The more we walked, the more we leaned to one side, about to fall over. By the time we were in the house, we landed on the couch before we fell over. We were both laughing and laughing until our sides hurt.

Have you ever noticed that when life starts getting too serious, even for just a moment, all of a sudden something silly pops into your head and you begin to smile just thinking about it? When you say what you're thinking about, you begin to laugh until your sides hurt or until you wet your pants, whichever comes first. After you've laughed, you don't remember what you were being so serious about. It is another way God shows us how much he really loves us and it will be okay, he has taken care of it.

Laughter realigns our eyes on Jesus and peace returns. When you live life too seriously, you're taking your eyes off of God and taking control. When you take control, you fall off track with no direction. The only way to get back on track is to ask God to take control once again.

Put your eyes back on God; he knows what's best for us. We don't, but he does. We think we do, but we don't—he does. That's why he is our father. He knows best. It's something to think about.

Once we stopped laughing, we both had lunch. Luke wanted to take a nap before the rest of the troop got home. We let everyone in on what the doctor said.

A few days went by, and it was time for Luke to go back to school. He loved school and didn't want to miss a thing. Luke was able to put weight on his foot when he needed to. He also had his portable wheelchair to get around in when he got tired.

Luke was to be in the cast for six weeks. It seemed like a long time, but the time went fast. Luke was really excited to get the anchor off his leg. The night after getting his cast off, he soaked in the tub with bubbles, and it made him feel better.

As time went on, we started to see Luke getting weaker and weaker each day. One day in particular, we knew his little body had changed dramatically, when he was trying to get out of his lift chair and his legs buckled under him and he landed on the floor. His legs couldn't support him any longer. It was a sad day to see someone who loved life and was outgoing and loved his independence. To see him on the floor looking up at you with tears in his eyes, knowing something had changed, was tragic. His legs were a lot weaker, and nothing was the same from that day forward.

We helped Luke off the floor and he said all he wanted was to go to bed. The next morning, Luke was complaining of his other leg hurting, so we wrapped his leg with an ace bandage to keep it tight—so it wouldn't hurt if he put any weight on it. Off to Longmont to the same place we took Luke the last time. While the nurse was looking over Luke's records, she noticed we were there just three months ago for the same thing. The nurse wanted to turn us in to social services for child abuse, since it was so close to the last time. I let them know that Luke had muscular dystrophy, but that didn't seem to matter.

If they didn't want to treat us, that was fine, and we left and went somewhere else. I know they were doing their job, but they could have handled it differently. We went to a place in Loveland, and the doctors fixed Luke right up. The doctors put one of those air casts on, where Luke could remove it for bathing. He needed to leave it on for six weeks like before.

While Luke still had his cast on, we had his appointment at Children's Hospital for his yearly check-up. We informed the doctors what had happened after the first cast came off after his surgery, when he broke his leg at the store—how weak it was. No sooner did he get out of one cast than he was in another. We didn't know how weak Luke was becoming until we saw it firsthand. We wanted to think Luke was fine as long as he was walking; we didn't want to give up on the chance he wouldn't need to go in his chair full-time. But the time was coming.

Then life gives you a wake-up call. During Luke's checkup, the doctors warned us of some of his upcoming challenges. Luke would be in his wheelchair for the rest of his life; the older he got, the weaker he would become. We didn't want to think that way at all, but it was something we needed to face. We took one day at a time, and we didn't let what the doctors said interfere with what how we lived our lives.

The six weeks flew by, and once again it was time to get Luke's cast off. The doctors wanted Luke to have water therapy to strengthen his leg to help him walk better. I remembered what the doctors had said in Denver. Before we put Luke through all that water therapy, we needed to talk to those doctors again, to see if this would help him. So I put a phone call in to Denver to see what they had to say. The doctors told me Luke could have all the therapy in the world and it still would not make his muscles any stronger.

Actually, they added, it would do more harm than good. Trying to make the muscles stronger would do the opposite—it would break down the muscle tissue and make him weaker. Luke's little body didn't have the gene you need to build up muscles to make them stronger. It would be like you trying to lift five hundred pounds by yourself—you just can't do it. Each day, a simple task like sitting on the floor or rising up out of a chair or writing his name with a pencil would become harder, and a simple stroll across the floor in time would be impossible.

His body would become weaker and weaker, and his legs would become unable to support him at all. Not only his legs, but in time all the other organs and other body parts would become weaker also. It was time to face what we thought was only a nightmare, something that would never happen. Indeed, Luke was going to be in his chair full-time.

There were lots of things we didn't know how to do, but everything worked out, and we all adjusted just fine. You know, God never gives us more than we can handle. Sometimes it seems hard at the time, but it isn't as hard as it seems to be. We didn't think how hard it was; we just trusted in what tomorrow would bring. Each and every day seeing Luke's happy smiling face made it seem a little easier to get through the hard times.

The day came when Luke asked why God made him the way he was. We are all special in every way possible, and God loves us very much. Each day we are being molded into the image of God. Not knowing it at the time, we are. He loves us all. Every trial we face and every mountain we climb are lessons we need to learn.

To keep growing and receiving all your gifts to be given, you will receive trials and mountains you have to climb to get to the other side. Keep your faith and love alive through the love you share with others. God chose us to bless us, not to hurt us—to help us every step of the way. Because God loves us so much, he blessed us with Luke. He knew in our hearts we had what it takes.

The largest tasks you are given in life are the biggest blessings you receive from God's hand. The gift of love is the best gift of all, the love you receive all along. Your tasks are stepping-stones of life that have been given to you. The cards you have been dealt are blessings. The best gifts of all are the loved ones you receive; you are blessed indeed. No matter what curves life throws at you, when you truly open your heart, you will see that the biggest blessings of all are the love we share with others and the love left behind.

In my heart, I had lots of anger. Why was this happening right in front of me and there was nothing I could do to fix it? I could only watch it happen, blaming myself. When you can't fix something, you start getting upset with yourself for not being able to fix it. It's not right to stay mad at yourself for something you had no part of. It wasn't your fault. It was best for me to forgive myself for something that was out of my control and wasn't my job to fix.

Although I didn't realize it at the time, I think this hidden anger made me stronger when it was time to use it. The hard lessons learned are the ones that have the most meaning behind them, to make you grow to the person God wants you to be.

If you don't grow, you go nowhere. That's no place to be, and there's nothing to see. Keep growing and learning and seeing all there is to see. Through your heart, with love, you'll see it the way it needs to be. Open your heart to see it and receive it.

Let go the things you cannot change from yesterday. The love and the lessons learned, take with you to look back on and visit now and then. Learn from them, pick up the pieces, and move forward. Keep doing the best you can and keep on loving along the way.

Each day, put a smile on someone's face, just like Luke did each and every day. Life is too short to live with mountains of regret. Forgive yourself over the things that you are unable to fix, knowing you did your best. You gave your heart and soul to what you know in your heart you are supposed to do. That's all God says to do—give your all. You do your part and he'll do his. Live life to the fullest and no looking back to try to change something that has already taken place. Keep looking forward, doing your best.

Each day is something new, and you gain wisdom through each thing you learn. Wear a smile as you walk a mile and put smiles on others' faces.

CHAPTER 11

The New Wheels

It was time to go back to Denver for Luke's checkup and also to check into getting sized for a power wheelchair. Luke was all excited that he could go anywhere without being pushed by someone else. With more independence, Luke could be cruising up and down the countryside. So we set his appointment to get his chair ordered. Luke was so excited that he got to pick out the color and some added features on the chair we ordered. It seemed to take quite a while for Luke's chair to come. It was like waiting for a brand-new car; to him, that's what it was.

The day finally arrived. Luke's wheelchair was delivered by a gentleman who worked for the wheelchair company. He spent the whole afternoon with Luke, making sure the chair worked out for him. All the adjustments were made, inside and out. Both of them went around the block several times. This man really cared, and it showed. But the next time we called up, he was gone.

Luke had a lot of fun in his chair. He cruised everywhere. The kids really helped Luke with the doors, his lunches, and all sorts of things he needed. This school year, the field trip was to Rocky Mountain National Park. The kids were so excited. The budget had been cut, so they were going to have to drive minivans. But Luke's chair wouldn't be able to fit, so they got hold of the bus barn and made special arrangements with one of the minibuses with a lift. Off to the park Luke went for a day of fun. He talked about it for days.

The time came to visit the middle school Luke would be attending. He saw his classroom, and he was a little nervous about the change that was coming around the corner. It was going to be a real adjustment for him without Dee Ann Wilson right down the hall. The teachers were trying to make the transition go as smoothly as possible, but it was still hard to say good-bye and let go of a place you had been accustomed to for so long.

I had also grown accustomed to where he was at. That is how life goes, though; everything changes, nothing stays the same. There is always something new to discover and learn each and every day of our life's journey. That's exactly what we did from that moment on.

That summer while Luke was at camp, George built him a new ramp as a surprise. It would be easier for him to get in and out of the house. We even painted the frame to match the house, and the main part was metal painted black to withstand the weather. It turned out great, and Luke was so excited when he saw it.

At the middle school, Luke was the first student to attend in a wheelchair. The school really needed to make some modifications to accommodate him. They forgot to modify the bathroom, so he ended up using the nurse office. It was hard for Luke as the new staff adjusted to his needs throughout the day. Luke was a trouper, though, and he went along with most things and let them know if he needed something. Luke attended that school for two years before we moved to Loveland after our finances hit bottom and we lost the house in Berthoud.

It was a change for the whole family and devastating at first. You think this is the end as you are going through it. It was one of those stepping-stones in life when you trip and fall and you get right back up again. In the beginning, it is hard, and in the end, you look back and see that it was the best thing for you.

When one door closes, another one opens. That's when you grow the most. You get to start again and don't look back, just keep moving forward. The move to Loveland was the best thing for all of us; it was a positive door. The kids made new friends in the neighborhood where we moved, and we did the same, forming everlasting friendships for all of us. We are so blessed that God put us in the right place at the right time.

At our new home, the church was so close it was within walking distance. God is closer than we think, and he has a hand in everything.

But we don't see that at the time, only what is going before us. Sometimes God plans it that way so we don't get too far ahead of his plan and take over. He puts roadblocks up so we have to lean on him to get back on track.

God knows we will make mistakes, and he will help us through them when we ask him to. God is helping you behind the scenes as he guides you through to the other side. You will grow a little more each time you cross that mountain one more time.

We moved into a condo in Loveland; at the time, it was the only thing we could find. I think living in a closer space brought us all closer. Luke stayed at my mom's, and they had some one-on-one with each other. It was a learning experience for the two of them.

Luke enjoyed showing her all the ropes and all the love he had for everyone who was dear to his heart—a smile and a loving and caring spirit he shared with everyone he met. Luke always had something to say that made you feel special, and he always saw the good in people. Luke's sense of humor was like no other. He was always laughing and looking at life, saying, "Lighten up, it will be okay."

CHAPTER 12

The Condo

Before we could bring Luke into the condo, George needed to build a ramp so Luke would be able to get in and out. It was a very complex ramp with hinges, and you had to lift up and down. Luke's bedroom was the living room on the main floor right off the kitchen, next to the TV room. We made do with the space we had—it was an adventure, like a giant sleepover that lasted a year. That was our goal that it was only going to be a year. Therefore, we made the most of it.

It was time for school to start once again, and this time it was going to be a new place and a new school. The first day at Walt Clark, we met with the teachers Luke and Latisha would have, and they were very nice. Latisha at the time was in sixth grade and Luke was in eighth grade. In Luke's class, the kids were able to call the teachers by their first names, and that made it easier for the kids to remember on a daily bases.

Luke really started to blossom among the new places and faces. His trust was strengthened each and every day by all the loving and caring people. It really showed in the way he talked and acted toward others and the love he gave.

Luke was also exposed to not-so-nice people, and he had God's grace and strength to be able to handle all the things that came his way. I know it was sometimes hard for him, but he was quick to forgive. He always looked for the best in others, never judged a book by its cover, and always saw what was in the person's heart. He knew if you had a good or a bad intention before you even said a word.

Luke's encouraging words were ones that you wanted to hear, and they were intended to help you, not to hurt you. When you took a moment and really listened to what he had just told you—not just stomp off in a fit and be mad for a while—it was hard to admit at the time but he was right. We would usually laugh about it and move on. Luke would let you know if your outfit looked good and if he liked your new haircut and it looked nice on you. He would always have a positive response with a little giggle that made you rethink your idea.

Luke had his own way of keeping his sister grounded. He loved her and let her be herself. He listened to her and allowed her to vent when life threw her a curveball that she had not been expecting. In life, we have a lot of yelling and a lot of misunderstandings and growing pains to go around. Sometimes the less you say, the more you are heard. Look around you, see what you see, hear what you hear, and learn from it.

Luke's advice was wise beyond his years when he would tell you what he thought or what not to say. He did a lot of listening and watching and learning. In life, that is a wise thing to do. Some of us should say less and listen more. We need to accept what we cannot change. Let it go and move on when hard things cross your path.

Luke started getting sick. We took him to the hospital and the doctors did an ultrasound on him. At the time, they thought he had an infection and sent him on his way home with a prescription to be filled. That night and on through the morning, he began to get worse. In my heart, I knew that we needed to take him down to Children's Hospital and have them look at him. Thank the Lord we did, because he needed to have emergency surgery.

The following day, he was sent home to recover. While Luke was home, the kids in his class made him get-well cards. Those cards meant a lot to him—the kids really missed him. It was like one of the puzzle pieces was missing when one of the kids was gone. All the kids were a big part of the class, and their love for each other was very strong. They all had a special bond with each other and the teachers too.

The special love for each other was real and true. The kids honestly knew what true love was without even trying. In their hearts, they knew love was as natural as breathing. It was sincere and genuine—the real thing, no buts about it. Some of us could only imagine a special love like that.

Let go of what you think love should be. Love yourself just the way you are, because we each have our own specially designed blueprints. You aren't supposed to want someone else's blueprints. Why would you want someone else's blueprint when you have been given your own? You know in your heart you have love deep inside when you look real close.

Love yourself, and your whole being will revolve around how you treat yourself. It will affect how you treat others. What kind of love do you see? Let your hair down and be your wonderful self, who God had intended you to be. Who else would qualify to be you but you? Why not be all you can be?

Think back to when you were a child, when you were too young to hate and love was there. You knew in your heart it would be there once again. Look in your child's eyes and you will see what they see, and that is love—the real love that comes from above. Open your heart to see and feel the love—the choice is yours to love and to be loved.

Starts today don't put it off until tomorrow. Tomorrow never comes. Live in the moment—the moment that is here and now. When the moment is gone, it is gone. Make it count while you are in it. You will not regret a thing. You will have enjoyed the whole journey through.

Luke was well enough to go back to school. The kids were excited to see him in class again—the puzzle was back together once more, just in time for a field trip to the Stock Show in Denver. The whole class got to see the animals up close. It was a lot different seeing them in person than seeing them in books. There were also baby animals for the kids to pet. The kids and the adults had a great time. When the kids got back to school, they drew pictures of all the animals they saw.

What I remember most about Luke's experience at the Stock Show was making sure he did not drive in the cow manure. Luke was really particular about his chair; he really appreciated what he had and wanted to take care of it. It was his transportation, and he was very thankful and grateful for it.

All Luke ever showed was love, and that is all he needed to do. That was his sole purpose, and that's exactly what he did. Luke did not care what others thought; he did his own thing. He was himself, and he did not change for anybody. He knew what was in his heart and did exactly that.

Spring was now upon us, and it was time for Luke's birthday party. It was a little gathering with a few friends from his new neighborhood and a few from Berthoud. Luke's cake was a racecar; it was so neat and tasted great too. After we all ate cake and opened the gifts, it was off to the movies. We saw *Volcano*. The day was filled with fun, laughter, and lots of memories that we will never forget. When we think back, we will remember all the fun we had and the love we shared.

CHAPTER 13

On the Move Again

It was time for Luke to visit high school. Where did the time go? The eight years of school went by in a flash, and now Luke was on his way to another one. Going to high school meant making another transfer, with new teachers and new surroundings.

At the end of his eighth-grade year, Luke's class had a little assembly. It was like a mini-graduation for the kids going to high school with certifications. It was a fun, joyful day with lots of memories the kids would remember for a long time.

We knew Luke couldn't handle another summer in the condo without air-conditioning. Therefore, we started looking for another place to live. On the first morning of summer vacation, we were driving in a new neighborhood and saw a for-rent sign in a window. Come to find out the lady had just put the sign in the window that morning. She was in the process of cleaning and painting the house for the new tenants who would be moving in. She invited us in to look at the house, and once we saw it, we knew it would work for us. The arrangements were made to set the deal in motion. Our prayers were answered.

When the date came for us to move in, Luke was at camp and I was away on business. It was up to Latisha and George to pack and move this time. The two of them were up for the challenge. It took some doing, but they got it done. It was such a blessing to come home and all I needed to do was start putting things away.

By the time Luke arrived home, his room was all set up and waiting for him. We had a few glitches to work on, but we got them all worked out. I needed to leave on another business trip for which I would be gone a little longer than the last time, so I needed some reinforcements to help. I was so grateful when George's mom and my mom agreed to take shifts helping with the kids.

We started needing more help with Luke at home when he was in the wheelchair full time. A specially if I was gone or if George was at work. Latisha helped her grandmas and her dad throughout the week on the daily route. In the evening, the aides would come back and help Luke back into bed. It worked like a well-oiled machine; it was a blessing. Later, Luke told me he was glad that I was home. George and Latisha were as well.

In the new neighborhood, the kids ventured out to meet new people. Luke met some who were into hotrods, motorbikes, and other cars. Whatever they were working on, they made Luke a part of, such as tearing down an engine or painting a new motor after it was ready to be put back in the truck. Luke's eyes lit up from the start. When George worked on a car, Luke was always there to help and remind his dad about missing items, such as a spring or a bolt or two.

Luke's advice would always have logic behind it. There was a day when his dad was in the front yard looking at the landscape, getting ready to prune the rosebushes back. Luke talked to his dad about this dead rose with its stem and leaves still attached to it. The rose represented the road of life. The stem was the main road of life, and the thorns represented the trials and struggles you have in life. The leaves were little rest areas that you could pull off on to rest for a while. Then you got back on the road to travel some more, until you got to the next leaf and pulled over to rest again. Eventually, someday, you would reach the top.

George asked, "Luke, what does that mean?"

Luke said, "It is heaven."

"How do you know?"

"Jesus told me."

"When did you talk to Jesus?" George asked.

"Jesus talks to me all the time," Luke replied.

His dad said to Luke, "Have Jesus talk to me!"

Off Luke went on one of his adventures. As he rode away, his dad stopped and stared in amazement. Luke knew he had nothing to worry about it. He knew where he was going, and Jesus was leading the way home.

On one of Luke's adventures, he got his chair stuck in the sand over by the school. From our house, we couldn't see what was happening. The neighbor next door saw and ran over to help him get unstuck. We were so thankful the neighbor was home and acted so quickly. From that day on, Luke never went close to the sand at school.

Each day, he went visiting with his new friends and had fun with the things they were working on. Luke came home one day with a new story about how he saw them take a motorbike apart and put it back together after it was all painted and how it shined. With the details he would tell, it was as if you were right there with him.

Luke had other friends on the other block. It was a young family with little kids. Every now and then, they would invite Luke into their home for a cool drink and to share their love with him. I was so grateful that there were people in the world who shared love and kindness with others.

In addition, Luke was around some not-so-nice people. When that would happen, his kindness would still be there. Down the road, the seeds he planted through kindness would grow in their hearts. We were always grateful to see the kindness others showed toward Luke, the boy in the wheelchair who passed by their path in life. Today, I know God has blessed them in so many ways by the love and kindness experienced by the softening of their hearts with one seed.

That year in school, Luke met a mean person he could not reach no matter how hard he tried. He thought, "Oh well, move on," even though it hurt him. I really learned how Luke was so humble. The year he got first place in the mini-car derby in Boy Scouts, he didn't mention a thing. The only way we found out was when we saw his picture on the front page of the newspaper. We asked him why he did not tell us. All he did was grin from ear to ear.

Luke had all sorts of patience, more than you could ever imagine. He waited on doctors and aides for the items he used every day, and waited on his mom putting out all sorts of fires in the house that needed my attention. Waiting on a meal to be prepared or being dished up; a movie to start and a class to begin; his bus to arrive to go to school—whatever it might be, he passed all the tests of being patient. He was always concerned about others and not himself. He loved us all from the start.

Each test that life put him through helped him stand stronger in his faith. The harder it got, the stronger he got. Luke's heart sometimes grew weak, but his spirit was strong. He never gave up, he just kept marching forward. Luke had a trust that was bigger than words could explain. He lived in the moment and made every day count.

Luke had a lot of fun and never let fear stop him, whatever he set his mind to do. He believed and just went and did it. He did not care what others thought. He always lived life to the fullest with no regrets. He shared love with all who passed his way, always with a smile and a giggle or two. The laughter made everything a little brighter and clearer, and joy filled the air with all the laughter shared.

CHAPTER 14

Some Good, Some Sad

The stories that Luke lived, the fun that he shared . . . One time his class went on a fishing trip, and the whole class was catching fish all day, except Luke and his teacher Denise. He had more fun watching than catching fish. His enjoyment was watching Denise casting out the line and releasing the button. Laughing and giggling was what he loved to do most.

Luke didn't care if he caught a thing that day. What he talked about the most was laughing and giggling with Denise. Those two had a special bond—the buddy system. They shared life stories with each other. When Denise had her baby, Allie, she brought her by our house so Luke could see the little one and take some pictures of them. Those are memories they will remember for a lifetime.

The good times we had with the kids included ski fundraisers. This year, Luke was a little apprehensive about going, because he did not know who would be going to be with him for the day, which made him a little nervous. Denise and Tom his other teacher always had a plan that had Luke covered; they reassured him he would be taken care of, and that enabled him to relax.

I really think all the people who touched Luke's life were his guardian angels some way or another. He always felt safe and trusted the ones around him. This year, Joe went along and was Luke's partner for the day. The two of them went down the hill on a snow sled and had a ball—a little frozen, but happy. When Luke had enough of the cold, it was time to go inside for hot chocolate and lunch and then head back down the mountain for home. From the pictures with the kids and their smiles, you could tell they had a great time.

It was so nice, all the wonderful activities and all the fun the kids got to experience and to learn from. When it was time for them to visit the museum in Denver, Luke's chair had a malfunction and couldn't be fixed until later that day. Going to the museum was an adventure in itself. To get the chair to move up and down, we had to us a cordless drill with a special bit. We used it the whole time at the museum, and it was a nightmare. We both almost had a complete meltdown over it.

From then on, we made sure his chair was in complete working order before any more adventures so far from home. Come to find out later, the chair motor had a recall. That is exactly what we needed, because we keep calling them to fix it. The motor was faulty, and so we needed a new one.

You can't know what it is like, how devastating it can be when a wheelchair does not work properly unless you are the one who is in it. Think about it for a moment: it is like having a broken leg and no one is there to set it. You know that you can't walk on it or move without help. Same thing when someone's chair is down: it's like having a broken leg without a cast.

Luke always had a happy spirit, with a smile to share and a friendly word that made you feel special the whole day. No one can ever imagine someone full of so much life and love to give. It was heartbreaking to see someone with a loving spirit slowly deteriorating right in front of our eyes on a daily basis. We made the most of each day. Luke woke up ready to face the day with a smile—and a cracking a joke or two. He was a light in a dark place; he knew where he was going. Some mornings were full of laughter right off the bat, and some it took us a while to get the laughter going.

One morning, Luke had some loose teeth, so he decided to pull them out himself and hand them right over to us during breakfast. That was not the first time or the last; he did it each time he had a loose one. In life there is never a dull moment, always something new for you. It's hard at times with frustration and chaos going on all around. I could have gone negative on some things, but I chose not to go there.

Life goes on. You can't change things that have already happened. You can cry over spilled milk or you can go on, and that is what we chose to do. Some of our aides were like family and remain in our hearts forever, and they will never forget the love and the caring friendship and trust. Luke was a blessing to all who knew him; he touched them in such a wonderful way.

Even when things got hard and Luke grew weary and tired, the aides would come in with a smile to help Luke and make him laugh and have fun. Even though the days grew dark and the light grew dim as his journey and his race came to an end, the fire Luke had inside was not ready to go out. He had some living yet to do and things to accomplish first.

Luke liked surprises of any kind. On his eighteenth birthday, we decided to surprise him with a party at school. It was such a delight to plan. While the kids were out, we came in to decorate for the party. We also brought pizza in for all. It was doubly special because we met the Annis family for the first time. It was an honor to meet such a loving and giving and caring family. We are so blessed that God brought us all together. Our friendship has grown to be more like family. That's the way we hope it will always be.

Our boys had a lot in common. Both were diagnosed with the same dystrophy. Our families were able to relate to each other and understand more and shed some light on things—not knowing at the time how much we would need each other even more down the road. The one above knew.

We were glad everyone was able to make it to the party. Especially the whole family Michael and Alison the mom and dad of the boys of Brennan, and Dillon Annis which the boys were class mates. At that time, Dillon was weak and very frail, but his spirit was strong and he was determined to attend the party. All the decorations were put in place and everything was set; the lights were off, ready for the birthday boy to arrive. He came up the ramp with no idea what was about to happen. The door opened and we all yelled, "Surprise!" Luke was so blown away he about fell out of his chair. The pictures Denise took were priceless.

Luke's face lit up and his grin filled his face. As his eyes looked around the room, he was so excited that all his friends were able to come to the class room and be a part of the surprise. Luke was so grateful that Dillon was able to attend. He knew how difficult it was for Dillon to go places. Luke went over to talk with Dillon and his family, and he thanked them all for coming as he did with everyone else.

It was pizza time. Even though the kids just had lunch, everyone was still up for pizza. We moved on to gifts—all the kids brought presents, it was so cute. The kids all shopped and picked out the gifts and wrapped them for the party. Luke loved everything that he received from everyone.

We sang "Happy Birthday" to the birthday boy and had some cake. That whole day, Luke was on top of the world and having such a great time, laughing and giggling with all his friends and having fun living in the moment, not worrying about tomorrow but living for today.

Keep this in mind: have fun right where you are. The memories you make will last a lifetime. It was such a fulfilling day, remembering it to this day still brings a smile to my face.

CHAPTER 15

A Friendship

I am with you even though you don't see me. I'm here with Jesus, where there is no sorrow or rain or pain. It is so beautiful, more than you could ever imagine, the love and peace we all share. Think how wonderful it is when you see a summer sunset from the mountains to the sea, every new baby you see and every new day.

Remember me; it will fill your hearts with love that we shared. We will be reunited in a little while. With all the angels running and jumping and laughing and singing with Jesus and all the fun we will all have? The warmth and joy you feel in your heart when you think of me and the stories you remember and the fun we had and the fun yet to come. When we all are together once again with Jesus it will be a joyful reunion.

Fill your hearts with love knowing where I am at. I'm in good hands running and jumping and having the time of my life, waiting for you. I love you see you soon, love you take care. Enjoy your journey, like I enjoyed mine, especially with all the love and care you gave me. Heaven awaits you, when you get to heaven it is more than you could ever imagine. Keep believing and keep love in your heart as I did. Even when times get tough as we know they can. Stay positive, no matter what. The reward is above and beyond what you could ever imagine. Keep pressing forward. The light will shine again, even though it seems so dark right now. Each time the sun shines on your face and you feel the warm rays or the cool breeze upon you, it's me. That will ease your mind. I'm closer than you think, even though it seems I'm so far away.

Memories that you have in your heart will keep me even closer. You can view any time the love and fun times. That is a blessing and a gift from above. Another miracle from God that I know is true. Bless everyone always . . . spread love and see all the joy it will bring. It starts with one. As Jesus loves us all that we can keep the chains of love going. Remember, all things are possible with God!

—Love, Dillon

Thinking back on this day, it was a celebration of Dillon's life and his journey going home. It was time for God to call Dillon home, God needed him home. He is safe in Jesus' arms knowing where he is. There were tears and stories that were shared that made you laugh and cry, knowing the love they shared with each other.

A strong and dear friend, his love touched our hearts, but he had been called home. His journey here on earth was short, but his time had impacted many. The love he gave others, his brother and his sister and his mom and dad, would last more than words can say here on earth. You felt in the soft-spoken words to your heart some reassurance that it would be okay.

The pain he suffered here when he left for paradise outweighs the pain down here for the ones who were left behind. We knew in our hearts that he had no more pain to bear down here. It hurt us all more to see him hurting and in pain all the time down here daily, when there was nothing you could to make it better, no matter what you did. But in the end, you did your best to make him as comfortable as you could; while he was in so much pain, that's all he ever asked. That was exactly what you did—you did your best, and God took care of the rest.

God never gives us more than we can handle, even when we think it is too much and we could not handle another thing. We get right through it, even when it seems too hard. We get up and do it all over again the next day. It makes it worthwhile every day when we see the love and the trust in their eyes, the way they keep smiling even when they are in so much pain. The only thing you can do is keep your focus on them. If not, you will begin to fall to pieces.

It is best not to think too much about what is really taking place right in front of you. The best thing is to savor each and every moment, make it fun and exciting and joyful as you can. Life is too short to put such high expectations on yourself; it gets you you-know-where. The only person you end up hurting is yourself; let it go. Know in your heart you did your best, and the love you shared and the memories will remain. Leave the expectations up to God; he will never let you down. Thinking you needed to do more is nonsense. You did what you needed to do.

Our boys knew the love we had for them and the love they had for us; the connection, the bond, will last forever. In your heart, you know the hurt and the pain they endured throughout their lives. They would go right into the arms of Jesus, where there was no more pain or rain and no more wheelchair adjustments forever. They would be running and jumping and laughing and singing peaceful melodies with all the angels.

Everything is sunny and bright with no darkness in sight; you see the streets glowing of gold and jewels sparkling bright. Think happy thoughts with your heart. The more you see, the more you begin to realize what matters most and the things that don't matter at all. The love you give will see you through. Take time to make time to listen to your kids—you can learn so much. When Luke told me it was going to be his turn to go home, I replied, "Don't think that way," but I knew deep down he was right.

We didn't focus on it. We kept looking ahead and moving forward. One step at a time, putting one foot in front of the other.

Life always seems to be in a rush; nothing ever seems to get done. Even though days are tough and rough seeing what is going on right in front of you, know in your heart God gives you the strength to go on even when you don't think you can. Yes you can, by not thinking what is going on as the days go by. Make each day fun and enjoyable as best you can.

Luke and Brennan had a friendship that grew stronger and closer each day. The last two years that Luke went to the Easter Seals camp, the boys were in the same cabin. At camp, the kids had their own counselors. They got to enjoy a lot of different things, including a lot of guy talk with other campers.

At camp, it was always fun, living in the moment and experiencing everything. Laughing and joking, fishing, swimming, playing ball, and firing off homemade rockets were among the activities they enjoyed. They watched all the Harleys arrive and met all the riders and took pictures with the riders. One time Luke even got to ride on one of the Harleys before all the changes came about that no longer allow them to do so.

The last night at camp, there was always a dance. It was so sweet, the awards each one of the kids got. They had one whole week to not worry about the outside world; they were able to come alive and do whatever their hearts desired. During the week, there was a video made for the local TV station to air during the Jerry Lewis telethon in September. Pictures were also taken with the whole group of all who were there that week. Then the pictures were sent home so the kids could look back and remember all the fun they had.

Camp week always went so fast for the kids; it seemed they just got there and it was time to go home. Everyone said their good-byes. We loaded up for our venture back down the mountain for home. We loved to hear the stories Luke would tell about his camp adventures.

Luke's last counselor was a very tall man from Kenya. He told Luke stories about where he was from and where he was attending college, and all the fun he was having here being Luke's counselor this week. We arrived back home and unloaded the van and then unpacked Luke's suitcase. As soon as he got home, he wanted to visit his friends and tell them about the fun he had.

The following week after Luke arrived home, the folks from Foothills Gateway from Ft. Collins came by. We talked about having an aide go out in the community with Luke to have fun and do some different activities. It would be like a friend who would come and take him places and hang out from time to time. Luke was all for it; he got to choose who he wanted.

It started out with aides from Luke's school who he knew real well and then moved on to ones he got to interview to take their place. Some worked out and some didn't, and that was okay. There was always a new one who worked out just fine and stayed until it was the time of the season for change and the person moved on. Life has its seasons for change so we can grow and learn from someone else who has been brought onto our path.

The girls who passed through Luke's life touched him in so many different ways. Some were friends, some were teachers, and some were helpers—some more than others, from elementary to middle school all the way up to high school and beyond. Others just wanted to be there to help in some way or another with lunches, with his chair, and with opening the door. To fix anything that he needed to have fixed or wanted fixed, the girls were there. Some drove him crazy, some were a delight, and some were all right. But all in all, he made them feel special no matter what, and they were all friends. Luke cared for them all. He would ask about them when they were not in school.

Luke would ask about the others kids too if they were absent. When the kids would return, he was concerned for them, to see how they were today. Luke cared about everyone; he knew when you were down. He had that special blessing—he could turn someone's sad day into a happy and positive one with just a few simple words.

It wasn't so much the words he said but how he said them that made the difference. His words touched you in a special way. He would take your frown and turn it upside down. The smile he would bring to your face would brighten your whole day.

Always try to remember to say an encouraging word to someone who is down with a frown. See what a difference it will make. A smile will remain with just one word and a brighter and lighter day that had started out dark from someone's remark. You can turn their day around with an encouraging word and a smile that will last a while. Try it and see it begin to work.

CHAPTER 16

Senior Year

It is Luke's last year of high school. He was a senior—where had the time gone?

Shortly after the start of the school year, Luke started not feeling well, so we took him over to the hospital. We were sent to Children's Hospital in Denver. He was admitted for about a week; he had a severe kidney infection that required IV antibiotics, something that was strong enough to knock it out. Plus Luke needed a lot of fluids because he also was dehydrated. When Luke was released from the hospital, he needed to continue his IV treatments for the rest of the week. Then he got to go to pill form to finish the rest of his treatment.

Once he was up to it, Luke wanted to go back to school. Luke absolutely loved school and all the daily adventures. It was a lot of fun with the whole class. Luke knew his limitations, and he was up for any adventure within reason. If he was not into it, he would tell you, but he was always willing to try something at least once.

We all need to know our limitations but be willing to try something new at least once. You only have one life; don't live in regret. Why not try it? You might even like it! You have nothing to lose and everything to gain by trying something new. Confidence will take you places when you are bold and experience new things, once you step out and do something you have always wanted to do. Not only talk about it, but really go out there and do it. That's when the real journey begins, and it will take you farther than you could have ever imagined it would.

Start today with a can-do attitude and see where it will take you. Let the Lord guide you; he will never leave you or forsake you. That's all you need to remember—he will be with you every step of the way. With the faith of a child, we know that we will be well taken care of, no matter what. When we get older, why do we let fear in and let faith go? We need to keep faith in and let fear go.

When you keep your faith, you will begin to grow and to know, and it will show. You are still a child of God, even when you grow up. Remember that.

Luke knew where his strength came from, and that never changed, it only grew stronger, by the way he lived and all the little things he would say. It would impact you in a big way. God thinks about us more than we think he does. He loves us more than we think. That needs to be shared with others, to encourage others every step of the way. That's why Luke got up every day with a smile on his face; he knew where his strength came from. He loved to share it with you in every way possible.

One of Luke's favorite things to do was watch movies. Every Friday night was pizza and movie night. We would rent more than one movie, so then it would carry over through the rest of the weekend. We had a whole movie collection of our favorites here at the house to enjoy as well. Luke enjoyed having his own TV in his room so he could watch movies after he went to bed. You would ask Luke about a movie he saw a month ago, and he could tell you the whole scoop, if it was good or not or if he had seen it or not.

Luke loved his action movies and Westerns, especially the ones with John Wayne in them. Luke and I would even watch love stories and movies that would make us both laugh until we cried. The movies we liked best were real-life stories. When others were around, such as Latisha and George, we sometimes would watch what they wanted to watch. The two of them were really flexible on what they watched, though. We all had fun and enjoyed whatever was on.

At the time, Luke's sister was at the age where she wanted to talk on the phone and boys started to come into play. It was more important than what was on TV. Luke would listen to his sister talk on the phone and knew what was going on all the time. The stories, he kept to himself. Luke only told if it was going to help her—like the time when his sister tried shaving for the first time and cut her thumb on the blades.

Thank God he did, because it really needed to be looked at and properly wrapped up. Otherwise, Luke never told on her. He encouraged her to be all she could be. Luke loved his little sister and knew how special she was—what a terrific lady she was becoming and how bold and confident she was. In his own way of doing things, no matter where he was going or what he was doing, he always thought of her.

Luke always remembered to bring something back for her or include her in what he was doing—especially the time he got to ride in the fire truck. The fire guys asked Luke where he wanted to go, and the first thing out of his mouth was, "Swing by my house and pick up my sister." So off they went and stopped by the house to pick up Latisha so she could ride too. Their smiles glowed for miles. You could tell they had a special bond from the start, and their love for each other grew and grew. As they got bigger, their bond got stronger and lasted longer. No matter what came against them, their actions told the story.

There was no need for words; sometimes words just get in the way of how it really is and how it will always be. Love speaks louder than it appears to be seen or heard. What is in your heart comes out to be shared with others, like two angels looking out for each other. As the kids got older, they even looked out for each other more than ever before. If one wasn't where he or she was supposed to be, the other would go looking. The love was always there no matter what, and that's the way it would always be.

Each time Luke was in the hospital, his sister was there to make sure he was okay in every possible way. She would even set the nurses straight on some things as well, to make sure his care was top notch. One time I was on overload at the hospital (not our regular one). No one would listen as I was trying to let them know what was going on with Luke. I was about to go out in the hall and have a screaming fit all by myself. I walked out into the hall, and that's when God sent his little intervention. Latisha was coming down the hall, and our paths crossed. "Please go in there and take over," I said, and she knew exactly what to do. Did it with no questions asked. It was all settled by the time I got back into the room. In life sometimes you need a time out, and that was one of those times.

I found out the hard way trying to be supermom that's its okay to make mistakes. The mistakes you make the hard way are the experiences you learn and grow from and remember for a lifetime. It is okay to make mistakes; no one is perfect, and we shouldn't pretend that we need to be. No one expected me to be supermom, but in my mind, I thought I needed to be to make everything all right. I didn't have time for mistakes or do-over's, I thought. I couldn't wait on anyone else to make a mistake either. So I did it all myself—or I would do it over after someone had all ready done it. I had to do it to make sure it was perfect.

It was too much. By doing that, I made more work for myself than I needed or wanted. It's okay to trip and fall and make mistakes from time to time. That's how you learn and grow. That's how and why you learn the hard way. You know what they say: yesterday is gone but not forgotten. The lessons learned are stepping-stones for tomorrow.

You can't change what has already happened, but you can sure pick up the pieces and go on. I did my best, and that's good enough for me. That's all God expects from me. That's the way it shall be.

Luke loved and accepted himself. Luke loved and accepted and loved me exactly the way I was, no matter what. That's exactly what he showed each and every day, even when I was supermom trying to make everything perfect for everyone and trying to fix everyone who needed to be fixed, even when they didn't need it at all.

Learn to laugh more—it makes the day go better. Even when it seems so dark, laugh louder, and the lighter it gets and the more at peace you feel as joy fills your heart. Try it sometime, it really works. Remember, it isn't the end of the world if you make a mistake. It is the end of the world if you don't make a mistake. Think about it. You learn so much by the mistakes you make. In your life journey, you will have many hills to climb and mistakes to make, and you learn from your mistakes.

Think of mistakes as little hills: you get back up and get ready for the next hill to climb. Enjoy the journey. We all are one; you are not the only one. Why not have fun and enjoy your life along the way? Life is like a carnival ride—some rides are fun and some are not. How you enjoy the ride is the most important thing.

CHAPTER 17

Graduation

It was time to make plans for graduation. We decided to have Luke's party at our church; it was quiet and peaceful. It was also close to Luke's school, and we could head right over for the festivities afterward. We really wanted it to be special for Luke. We were so proud.

The beginning of the week of his graduation, it was snowy and very cold. By the weekend, it was just right. The snow had melted on the field and the surroundings, and that made it a lot easier to get around for Luke on his big day.

Luke had chosen Carrie Reed to go down with him to receive his diploma. Graduation started at 9:30 a.m. We were able go into the church hall the day before to set up for the party, and that made it wonderful for us.

The big day arrived, and we all were so excited and a little nervous. We put Luke's cap and gown on. He looked so grown-up. Before we left for the school, we took pictures, and then when we got to the school we took more pictures. We also put his graduation on video from start to finish and throughout his party as well.

The memories of that special day will not be forgotten, and we can watch it from time to time. Luke's day was fun, and a lot of his classmates came for his celebration party. The two teachers—the one who started his school journey with him, Dee Ann Wilson, and the one who took him through his high-school years, Denise Regalman—both had a little something to say about Luke and how he impacted their lives, the things he taught them while they were teaching him. The words that were spoken touched our hearts in a way that we will never forget. Others could learn from what a little love and kindness can do.

Luke's great-aunt told a story about how when Luke was little, her daughter Laurie was holding him and they were turning the light on and off. He was laughing and laughing the whole time while she was doing it. There were good memories, good food, and an all-around fun day. The ones who lived out of town sent their blessings and graduation cheer long-distance to make the day complete.

You know, sometimes things just happen, and this was one of those days. Earlier that day, right before the ceremony took place, Luke's gown hooked on his up and down switch and move forward too far. The impact was real hard. We asked Luke if he was okay, and he said yes. Even if he wasn't okay, Luke didn't want to miss his day for nothing.

As the day came to a close and we ventured back home, Luke was getting ready for bed, and his shoes were taken off. We were careful with his foot, as he was propped up like normal. It wasn't until the next day that we realized something serious had happened to his foot. We took him right over to the hospital for X-rays. Sure enough, it was broken. On went the cast for the whole summer. From that day forward, we made sure nothing came near that switch.

The cast didn't stop Luke from going to camp or any other activities he'd planned for the summer. When Luke got back from camp, he went shopping to spend some of his graduation money. Luke wanted a TV for his room with a VCR all in one. Luke really enjoyed going and picking it out and using it.

When it was time to go back and see the doctor about how Luke's foot was doing, the doctor said the cast needed to stay on longer; the foot wasn't healing like it should. Luke wore the cast all the way till October. It finally came off then, and Luke was a very happy camper.

In the meantime, we were on the move again. We located a house that we wanted to buy, so we put a bid on it. The house needed some work, and we had big ambitions. Our eyes were bigger than our pocketbook, and it was more work than we originally thought. We tried to make it work, but we realized that we'd bitten off more than we could chew. We stayed in that house for two years and moved on.

During our time in that house, we had a surprise eighteenth birthday party for Latisha. All of her friends and her brother were involved with the surprise—she had no clue. It was so much fun to surprise everyone now and then.

The day of her birthday, she was calling everyone to see if they wanted to come over and hang out, but everyone had plans. It was so sad to see her sad. I suggested she go out to lunch or something since everyone was busy, just to get her out of the house so we could decorate. We sent her on an outing with her boyfriend somewhere to keep her occupied.

By the time they got back, everything was set and ready to surprise her. As she walked into the house, we all yelled, "Surprise!" She was surprised indeed. All her friends were there, and she loved it.

The following spring, Latisha graduated from high school. How amazing—that time went by so fast, and now it was Latisha's turn. She was so grown-up. We had her senior pictures taken, and the photographer asked if she was a model. She said no, and he said, "Have you ever thought about it? You could. You have that special look, and you're easy to photograph."

We were so proud of both kids. We were so blessed that the Lord gave us two wonderful kids that we got to share our lives with. The door was open to walk through and see what dreams there were around the corner, what adventures lay ahead.

That year, Luke got a new respite-care provider to help out the other one. At that time, we had Laura and Tim come to help out and share the time Luke was allotted for. It worked out real well, because all three had a great time working together. Not all at the same time, but at different times, of course. Luke also went on to another program that followed high school; it was called Commuted Connection. That program lasted a year, and so Luke and Joanna his class mate also had her graduation. And Ron had a retirement party—he was Luke's bus driver.

The party was all in one. There were a lot of memories the both of them had together throughout the years. A video was made with them all through the years. Luke loved him and spoke often about him and all the funny stories about the daily bus ride to school and the field trips they went on. There were also stories about the aides Luke had on the bus, especially to make sure the kids in their wheelchairs were fastened tightly in place so they wouldn't go anywhere while traveling.

The kids were always happy laughing and having fun, never grim or dark, only joyful and full of light. What a delight and a treat! That is the way it should be; everyone is on a journey. Why not make the most of your journey and enjoy every moment of the day? It does no good to worry. It won't change a thing. Only your hair color seems to change when you do.

Next time you think you need to worry, look at children. You see them happy and enjoying life, living it to the fullest. Not a worry in the world, loving and caring and helping each other having fun. They know that they are covered; they trust and believe that they will be taken care of. So why worry? It's a waste of time. It gets you nothing but heartache and pain.

Keep believing and pressing on and running your race. It will get you to the other side just in time. Enjoy right where you are at. That way, you won't miss a thing, and everything is covered. You will never have regrets, only peace and joy and memories of all the fun you had and shared on your journey. Live in the moment right where you are at; right now is the best moment to start.

Watching the videos showed us that was exactly what they had done, by the look on their faces and the smiles and laughter they shared. Have more fun—it will take you more places to see more faces. The action is the writing on the wall. Even when you fall, you call. Not just reading the words or saying them—it's doing them that makes a world of a difference. Actions speak louder than any words, so put your actions to work.

See what happens; it only takes that first step. Keep moving forward one step at a time. Go for it! What do you have to lose? Nothing! You already have that. You have everything to gain. Go for it once and for all. The time is now—you can do it! Put your mind to it and go for it.

CHAPTER 18

Police Station

Luke looked forward to starting his position at the police station: office helper and paper shredder. He was so excited because he got to see other things and do other activities with Aunt Sally as well. Before Luke could even start, though, he had to have a background check. Then he had to be fingerprinted and a picture taken for his badge. The aides who went with him over to the station had to do the same as well. A short time later, a friend of Luke's from school got to work too. What was nice was that, as they worked together over at the station, they never got upset with each other. They helped each other like a well-oiled machine.

Think how nice it would be to work together and not get upset or mad when someone makes a mistake or two—to care more for each other's needs and wants. Too often we only care about our own needs and wants, and when someone doesn't fulfill them, we get mad and all upset. We need to let go of our high expectations. Something will always be wrong, no matter how high the expectations are. It is not other people's job to make you happy. Until you realize that and are willing to let it go, you will never grow.

Put all your expectations and trust in God and let the love in. It is all about what we can do for others and the love we can share. Today put a smile on someone's face. See how much joy you feel. See how happy you become when you stop thinking only about yourself and focus on helping someone else. The more you do it, the more your life will begin to change. That is the first step in trusting and believing God will fill your needs.

Take yourself off of your mind, and go help someone in need. That opens the door for God to work. The worry will be gone, and faith will show up. Do what you can do so God can do what you can't do. Each day, talk to God, look, and see how you can bless someone. The world will be a better place.

Just by looking around, you can learn so much. When you are talking to others, really listen—you will hear a need. If you have the ability to fill it then do it. If you are not able, find someone who can. When there is a will, there is a way.

Don't give up when obstacles get in the way. Keep pressing through to the other side. Then you let only positives flow out; it will encourage you as they come out. Words can build others up or tear them down. Think before you speak—the things you say can hurt or heal. You can learn by the actions that you see.

The good and the bad—God sees it all. You will be judged for it all. Think before you speak. The things we can learn from are in front of us. The writing is on the wall; take the time and see. The difference comes down to you and me. For the ones who choose to see, the time is now. Go for it before the time is up. Make the most of your journey, and enjoy it all the way through. Have fun and put a smile on someone's face as you run your race.

Luke and Michael worked together with Aunt Sally until she retired. Luke said, "Since Sally retired, I will too." And that is exactly what he did. About that time, Luke's aides were also ready to move on. You know how life is—everything changes for a reason. Nothing stays the same. It's a new season for some new faces to come in where the others left off. The ones who left after their season were touched in a special way they'll never forget.

God knows exactly the right time for putting others in—the ones who are strong and able to handle what life throws at them. I know that each one of us has a different level in our life that we need to learn from. Talking about learning new things—God gave us the opportunity to be in charge of our own home care, so that we would be able to hire our own aides and nurses. That way, we knew at all times who was coming and who was not. We were so grateful and thankful to the Annis family for helping us get hooked up with the program. It took a while for it to get all arranged, but once it was in place, it worked real well.

The summer after Latisha's graduation, she started working and learning what life is like out of school. She learned to be strong and bold and confident within herself, especially when she was sticking up for others and something she believed in.

Learning about love and living can sometimes hurt, and when it hurts, it makes you stronger. Love heals when the time is taken to let go and forgive all the harsh words that have been spoken. The action was taken when the heart was broken into. Sometimes a broken heart shows you what needs to be seen. When things are cloudy and dim, they are not what they seem to be. That is the only way to see when the heart is broken.

After you begin to see what you are able to feel, the healing begins when you accept and move forward from it. Each and every step taken is a lesson learned. Love and faith can move mountains, one step at a time. Kids are amazing; you think you haven't taught them enough, but you really have, judging by the actions they take.

That fall, Luke started complaining about his heart and not felling well at all. We went to the hospital to have Luke all checked out, and that's when they found out he had a serious infection. The only way he could be treated was by IV medicine. At the time, Luke's doctor asked him if something should happen to him, what would he want to do? "Whatever my mom says, I will be fine with it," he replied.

In my heart, I realized I didn't want to think this was the end. The more I did, the more it hurt, so I didn't think about it. I focused on the here and now, not on the things I couldn't change. Later he got better and was allowed to go home. All that mattered was putting a smile on his face, and he trusted that he would be taken care of.

Luke was so excited that he would be well for Christmas, because it was right around the corner. This year seemed a little different. Everything went so smoothly, with no glitches. It's awesome when things fall together like that. I think it was preparing us for something special around the corner. That's exactly what it was—a surprise. God pulled it right out of his planned layout manual. It was designed just for us, and it connected with the rest of the wonderful plan he had in mind for us.

We received a phone call from Latisha, right from the doctor's office. She thought she had a bad cold that she couldn't shake. While she was down there, it's so funny how God sends you in for one thing and you come out with a completely different outcome. That's what makes life a journey; you never know what to expect around the next curve. Go for it and be happy no matter what the outcome is. When you make the most of what life throws at you, the attitude you take makes a world of difference in how the outcome will play out in the long run.

God is always full of wonderful surprises. That day, when her dad answered the phone, Latisha had news: she was going to have a baby. Her father reassured her it would be okay. Latisha didn't know what our reaction would be.

"Dad, can you tell Mom for me?" she asked.

"No," he replied, "I will let you do the honor."

CHAPTER 19

The Big Surprise

As George handed me the phone, he said, "Grandma, it's for you." I was so excited, I could hardly contain myself. I was already talking about the baby shower and all the fun we would have. With a new addition on the way, I think Latisha was in shock at our response. The whole time, she was afraid of what our reaction would be; the response she got from others wasn't what she thought. But it made her think of what would be the best for her and the new life inside.

Others were concerned about the results back in the day, when Latisha was a baby herself, that she was a carrier and could pass the gene on to her babies. Since my grandmother and I did, the doctors wanted to rule out others. But at that time, the testing was so very new, it didn't have all the bugs worked out yet. At the time of Latisha's testing, she was six months old, so the test indicated she was a carrier. The doctor had said, "By the time she reaches childbearing age, there will be a more accurate test available."

All Latisha had to do was give some blood and then run it against Luke's tests that were done when he had a biopsy twenty years earlier. That's what they used to compare the results to; it was a DNA test. It was all in God's timing. The test needed to be developed first for future use. Now the wait would be over. The results had been long time coming.

Where faith has come down the line, blessings have arrived. It was the birthday gift I will never forget as long as I live—the phone call from Latisha letting us know that she wasn't a carrier after all. Praise God, it stopped with me; it was the most wonderful gift I could have ever asked for, knowing that Latisha's baby would be fine. Thank God. I was so grateful for all the wonderful blessings that I'd been a part of each and every day, and all the things and dreams that were yet to come.

When we first told Luke that his sister was going to have a baby, the first thing he said was, "No sir, it's just gas." We all laughed so hard at his response.

Luke was glad that his sister wasn't a carrier. When Luke saw the picture of the baby in the ultrasound, he told his sister, "Looks like you are having a head."

Latisha looked at Luke with a puzzled look on her face and she said, "A head? It better be more than a head."

Of course Luke laughed; he just said that to push her buttons and get a reaction from her. It was so awesome how Latisha and Adrian decided to name the baby Auston Luke after her brother when they found out the baby was a boy. Luke's face lit up, and he smiled from ear to ear. He really enjoyed that he was a part of the baby as a namesake, and he was a very proud uncle, that's for sure.

Each time he went shopping on one of his outings, he brought something back for the baby. One of the special things he brought was a little bank that was shaped like a monster truck that he painted himself with Auston's name on it. Then he sprayed it with shiny stuff. It was so beautiful. He wanted to surprise his sister with it the day the baby was born.

Things began to move quickly, like a whirlwind, too fast to keep your head on straight or think straight. We moved two times in six months. In life that happens sometimes, when you don't listen to that little voice that gives you wisdom. The first move, the place was over our heads and budget, and that's what our little voice was trying to tell us in the first place. But no, we did it anyway and learned the hard way. See what happens when you jump out and put the cart in front the horse? Then you have to go through a process to get out of the mess you put yourself in by not waiting just a little bit longer. That's okay; some lessons are needed to make us grow.

The second place we moved into, we listened to the little voice of wisdom a little more closely. It was just the right size and came available at the right time, and it fit into our budget as well. That is so awesome when that happens.

Between the first move and the second one, Luke got a new wheelchair that had a mind of its own, or so it seemed—especially the day Luke and his dad were in the garage talking and all of a sudden it jolted forward and ran straight into the bench. The chair pinned Luke up against the vise that was attached to the bench. When he got pinned, it was at Luke's throat. His dad quickly grabbed the chair and pulled it back; thank the Lord that his dad was there!

It scared us all half to death that his chair could do something like that. We found out later that sometimes cell phones going by in cars can cause things like that happen. We contacted the wheelchair place, and they came down to work all the bugs out. Thank God Luke wasn't seriously hurt. Thinking back to that incident, though, we often wondered if it had something to do with Luke's swallowing problems. If it did, there was nothing we could do about it. What's done is done, let it go and move on. What mattered most was that he wasn't seriously hurt.

The following week, it was time to go to Denver for Luke's checkup at the muscle clinic. The doctors wanted to see his new chair. We also told them about the news that Luke was going to be an uncle. The doctors and the staff were so excited for Luke and the whole family.

Luke's checkup went fairly well. The ride home was an adventure of its own. While we were driving on the interstate, the front tire blew out on the van. Thank the Lord George was driving. It was scary to be stopped on the side of the road. The van would shake back and forth each time the cars would blow by so fast. It didn't bother Luke at all, though; he was calm the whole time. I know his faith was strong, and it showed that afternoon.

The jack that came with the van didn't work properly. No one would stop to help; even the ones who were supposed to serve and to protect passed by. George even tried holding a sign to try to get someone's attention, saying that we had a wheelchair on board. It didn't seem to matter. You know when things don't work as easily as you think they should, there is always a reason. Luke kept saying to trust that someone soon would stop, and sure enough, the right time and the right moment arrived. The car that needed to stop at the right time and place had arrived.

"To pay it forward, to help someone in need," the young man replied when we asked why he had stopped, as someone had done the same for him when he was in need two weeks before in the same spot. That was so nice of him to stop and help us; he was an angel sent from heaven above. He swept down to help and was gone in a flash. Before we knew it, we were on our way home with the spare on and the blown-out tire in the back of the van.

As soon as we got home, George and Luke looked over the tire to see what had happened. Later they talked with a tire guy who informed us the others would do the same. It would be best to change all the tires at once. That's what we did, so we would have peace of mind on our next adventure in the van.

The following weekend, Latisha went into labor with Auston, at the crack of dawn on a Saturday morning. We were so excited for the new arrival. The two weeks leading up to the day, I slept with the phone by my side, waiting for her phone call. It was so exciting. Today was finally the day. The phone rang, and it was time to go off to the hospital. I sprang into action as the phone rang. George and Luke hung out at home waiting for news.

I did get to sneak home for a bite of lunch, and then I went back over. By the time I drove back to the hospital, it was time for the baby to be delivered. I arrived right on time to watch Auston being born. It was such an awesome experience—one of God's many miracles. You know God shows them to us all on a daily basis, if we really stop and look around. It is so amazing, all the details and all the beautiful colors in the sky. From the east to the west and the north to the south, there is so much to see. Each and every moment is something new to view, things to smell and feel and hear, especially a new baby's cry and a bird singing right outside your window on a summer morning.

When the evening sunset is fast approaching, the crickets and the fireflies glow in the distance of the evening shadow. Soon it will be morning again, flowers blooming, bees buzzing all around, the new buds waiting for the right moment to open to get the nectar out. Stop and take a moment to shut your eyes and take all the smell in after a spring shower. Feel a cool breeze gently gliding over your face on a hot afternoon. That's God you see.

Each and every day is a new experience. Our little gifts are given to us one by one, a little touch of heaven for each and every one. Enjoy them as you take them in; they are made especially for you. Take another look around and see God—all he has created, all the little miracles for you to enjoy. Take time and see and savor the moment, all the moments that take your breath away. That's exactly what I did the day Auston was born.

I was so grateful to have been a part of such an awesome experience, one of God's precious moments he shows us each and every day, the memories that remain after special moments are sent directly from him. They go straight to your heart and a sense of peace fills your soul. That is love; that's what matters most. Life is too fragile to live it as foolish game, being angry all the time, focusing on all the wrong things.

Start looking around. Life happens to all of us—let it go and move on. Don't focus on what has been done wrong to you but what has gone right. Focus on the right things and less on the wrong things, and your day will go more smoothly than you think.

When things happen in life, it's how you choose to handle it that affects the outcome. Your attitude means a lot—how you view things when they come against you, good or bad. If you have a bad attitude, you will hurt others and yourself over things you cannot change. Why get mad and all upset when things have already happened? It's a waste of time and energy, and you get to go around the mountain one more time.

Each day you take the same time until you pass that test. With a good attitude, it goes smoothly, and no one is hurt. What matters most of all is how you treat others; that is, love. Love is what matters most of all. Let love in and then you will let love out.

Look at all the babies in the world. Look in their eyes at the love wanting to come out and shine. Give love with a hug and a word that encourages and breaks off all the rubbish that covers the surface. When you do love, it goes in deeper than you think. God goes to work; you see what he can do. With one word and many words over time, it will pass on. The next hug and encouraging word is set forth by that first word.

You can make a difference with your first glimpse and your first words. Make a difference—it really works. Everything you do, walk in love, no matter what is going on. It will make a world of difference. You have a chance to walk in love every day; it's up to you to make that choice to walk in love. Let God's love in, let God's love out.

Kids love with all their hearts—the love comes and flows and it shows. Look at your heart, see if love flows and shows. You will know and others will know as love grows. The faith of a child is what God wants to see more of from you and me.

The first time I held Auston, we bonded instantly. After holding the baby, I called the house to let George and Luke know the good news. The phone rang and no one answered, so I left it on the machine. When George checked the message, he played it over and over for Luke. The new uncle's eyes lit up and were beaming, and he was grinning from ear to ear each time it was played for him. The both of them were ecstatic to go over and see the new arrival.

CHAPTER 20

The Light Will Shine Through

The next day George, Luke, and Luke's aide Amanda and I went over to see the baby. Luke was so excited to see his nephew and take the baby his gift. We got to the hospital, and his sister was so glad Luke and her dad came. Luke gave the gift to his sister that he made special for the baby—the monster-truck bank. Her eyes lit up; she thanked him and hugged him. The truck had Auston's name on it, and it was a blue marble color and very shiny. The whole day at the hospital, everyone put their change in it for the baby. It was so amazing to see Luke with the baby as we were helping him hold Auston. His eyes lit up and he grinned from ear to ear; he was so proud to be an uncle.

We took lots of pictures of us all holding the baby, and then we took a family picture. From that day forward, Auston was the center of our life, especially when he came over to visit or when we went over to see him to get our baby fix. Latisha would bring Auston over so Luke could spend some time with the baby as well. Also, we would have baby sleepovers when Mom and Dad had date nights. It was so cute how Luke and Amanda would go shopping for Auston. Luke was so proud to be an uncle; he talked about it quite often.

Amanda and Rob were Luke's aides they all shared fun times together doing various things through out the day. They were more like family and friends as well as his aides. There were days when Amanda wasn't available. Then Rob would come over and build models and various other activities. Luke really enjoyed both of them coming over. We really appreciated the time they spent with Luke.

A short time later, Luke started having difficulty swallowing. It really made it hard for him to eat certain foods that he loved. One of the days when Rob was over, Luke and Rob were having burgers for lunch, and Luke began to choke on one his bites. It was so frightening. We were unable to do the Heimlich on him in his chair. Praise God that when we hit him on the back a few times, it came out all at once. From then on, we were very careful about what he was going to eat.

Luke started to need oxygen more at night to help his heart not have to work so hard. As the disease started to progress even more, Luke's poor heart had to work even harder than ever before. To keep up, to help pump blood throughout his body, each day became a little harder than the day before. It was like overnight his little body frame got even smaller.

At Luke's checkup, the doctors suggested he needed to get an ultrasound to see how his kidneys looked so they could have a closer look, because Luke was having pain and a slight temperature and discoloration of his urine. After Luke's ultrasound, the doctors found several fair-sized stones in his kidneys that needed to be removed.

The doctors here in town thought it would be best if we went to Children's Hospital to see a specialist who worked with the smaller patients, because Luke's case was delicate. Soon as it could be arranged, we went to see the specialist. The specialist informed us he would have to operate and go in and blast the stones out. So we set a date prior to the surgery date. We needed to see other doctors to get the go-ahead to proceed with the surgery. We set up several appointments with various doctors to see if Luke's body could handle the surgery, and we got the go-ahead from all the doctors we saw.

Prior to the surgery, the clinic called to change the date. Instead of the fifteenth of December, it would be the thirtieth. At the time, I was all upset. Luke was going to be in pain longer than he should. But there is a reason for everything; sometimes it doesn't make any sense at the time until much later, when the time is right and the light comes on. That is the way it is supposed to be. Why get upset? It's a waste of time and energy. You can't change the way it's supposed to be—just go with it. It always works out for the best, even though it doesn't look like it right now. It always does, no matter what.

That year, Christmas seemed a little more special than before. In my heart, I thought it would be nice to get hold of Luke's teachers to come over and say hi. With it being Christmas break, a lot of them were out of town. The ones who were in town came over to see him. It was a good time for all.

After one of the outings Luke and Amanda went on, they brought me a beautiful bouquet of flowers. It was a wonderful surprise. It made my day and is something I will never forget.

Luke really had a special connection with the heavenly father. Several evenings we heard Luke talking to someone, and it wasn't George or I. He was talking to Jesus. It was a real heart-to-heart and soul-to-soul talk. It wasn't a person-to-person talk; it had a special sound, and it was a much deeper conversation. They were speaking in tongues. What a blessing to love and be loved by such a wonderful soul! It really showed how he lived and talked without saying a word. Luke had a special glow around him.

Babies felt soothing comfort when he entered a room. One day Baby Auston was crying, and we had tried everything to quiet him. Auston was wailing away in his bouncer seat on the kitchen table. Luke came around the corner in his wheelchair, and as he entered the room, the baby stopped crying. It was amazing to see what had just taken place. So you cannot tell me God doesn't exist, because he does. I saw God working through Luke that day and each and every day throughout his journey.

There are amazing things that go on day after day, if you just take time to look. From sunup to sundown and everything in between, your journey and mine have some good and some bad. You learn from both the good and the bad. You take bits and pieces with you each and every day to lead you to where you are going—to lead you back home.

Keep standing and pressing on, moving forward day by day, step by step? You will see the light on the other side. Enjoy your journey and the path; it has been designed especially for you. Everyone has a journey to go through. Have fun along the way and go with the flow.

Luke and I were watching a movie one afternoon. He asked me a question: "Why did you have me?"

I responded back to him, "Because we love you."

That night in a soft voice, I heard Luke talking to God as he was saying his prayers.

It was getting closer to Christmas day, so the kids came over to help us put up the tree. It was so much fun laughing and giggling, just like when they were little. This year, we decided to put ribbon on the tree to dress it up a little. With the balls and the lights, it was glittery and sparkling; in the darkness, it really glowed. The tree was just beautiful, and the baby loved the colors and the lights and stared at it with a smile on his face. We took pictures of the tree and Auston by the tree held by his mom.

A short time later, Luke wanted us to put Auston on the back of his chair to get a picture of the two of them. The picture is so cute—the both of them together on the wheelchair. We framed it plus the ones from the hospital holding the baby that we put up on the mantle so we can look at them any time. On Christmas Eve day, Grandma J. and Papa Frank came over so it wouldn't interfere with the kids' plans.

Lately, Luke had started getting up later in the mornings. On Christmas Eve morning, he got up and ate breakfast shortly before Grandma and Papa came. They spent time with all of us and left shortly before lunch. Luke seemed to be a little emotional around his grandparents; he didn't seem to be himself that day. Maybe he knew in his heart it would be the last time he would see them. His tears in the other room away from them were his silent way of saying good-bye to them.

A few days later, Luke said to me, "Mom, I need your help for the next two weeks, and then you can do whatever you want."

I didn't really fully understand what he was saying to me. "Of course I will take care of you," I replied.

In his own way, he was trying to tell me something, but I didn't know what it meant at the time. It would be revealed to me at later, but the words had been spoken. The gift that was given and the gift that was left behind was his love.

CHAPTER 21

The Surgery

All the doctors had given the go-ahead. The days leading up to the surgery included a trip to the ER with an irregular heartbeat, which alarmed us. It turned out to be okay after he was checked out. Two days later, we had Luke's pre-op appointment down at Children's Hospital. They checked him all over and said he was ready his surgery on Friday.

Surgery day we needed to be down there by seven in the morning. It was quite early to be up and on the roadway to be there before seven, but we made it. By the time the doctors came to take Luke back, he had been weighed and an IV put in. He gave us all hugs before he went in. We were all there and waiting to hear more in-depth what to expect before, during, and after the procedure. They also gave us this device that would go off to let us know the procedure was completed.

We all decided to go down to the cafeteria for something to eat. We thought we would have time to eat and be back before Luke's surgery was done. But just as we sat down with our food, the device went off, so we made a mad dash upstairs. The doctor explained what went on during Luke's surgery and why they weren't able to complete the procedure. The tool the surgeon used would go 90 degrees, but Luke needed it to go 180 degrees, and it was impossible to reach and finish the procedure. For right now, we needed to keep Luke as comfortable as we could until the doctors figured out the next step they were going to take. Opening him up and taking the stones out manually might be too much for his body to handle.

We didn't want to think about that right it now. We wanted to know how he was. We would think about the other options later, but right now Luke's condition took first priority. The doctor had put Luke in the ICU to recover. He needed to be watched and monitored overnight. Luke had his own private nurse to watch over him. Everyone came up to see how Luke was doing before they headed home. After everyone left to go home, it was just Luke and me.

Luke always liked for me to stay; he felt safe when I was there with him. This way I could rest knowing he was okay. We also had a special bond and a divine connection that I feel so blessed I got to be a part of. We were close, and I am so grateful. We learned so much about each other throughout the years and grew to trust each other.

Looking at Luke in his bed, it was really hard to see him in there. We were in a lot of hospital rooms throughout the years together. The beds were always uncomfortable some way or another, but we made it through. God always came through for us; it is his timing, not ours. This time was different. We were both at peace throughout the night. We had rock-and-roll oldies playing all night in our room. His bed was so comfortable, he slept all night long. Luke commented on it several times, how much he loved it and wanted to take it home with him. That was one of the best night's sleep he had ever had.

There was a calm feeling in the room. We both fell asleep after talking a bit with the nurse and each other. In the morning, when the doctor came in, he said that we could stay another day or Luke could go home. We decided to go home, thinking it was the best choice. When we arrived at home we realized we had no pain meds. I think the doctor figured we had some at home and that Luke could take what he was already taking.

In the middle of the night, Luke started getting more restless than normal. The next day, I talked to our family doctor to see if he could adjust the pain meds to get Luke something a lot stronger. The pain med he was on wasn't touching his pain level. That is when the doctor brought up the word *hospice* to come in to start giving morphine. I said, "No, let's try the pills first." I knew how much Luke didn't like change or interruption to the routine he was used to.

That is what we did to keep him comfortable—we tried the other pills. Those didn't touch his pain either, so we tried another kind. Finally we got the pills we should have had from the hospital. Luke started taking them, and it was making his pain worse. We couldn't figure out what was going on.

Things really started to change in a big way. Later that evening, George had a meeting in Denver, and Luke and I were home alone. Luke wanted to go to bed earlier and earlier each day. He only had a bit of energy per day. When his energy would run out, it was time to go to bed to get recharged for the next day.

When Amanda came over to put Luke to bed, she said, "If you need anything else, give me a call." I thought it would be a quiet night and Luke would get a real good night's sleep. Wrong: shortly after Amanda left, Luke called me into his room, and I stayed in there three hours adjusting and straightening him in the bed. No matter which way you fixed and straightened him, his pain got worse. He hurt everywhere on his body.

At that time, I was fried and exhausted, mentally and physically. Luke looked at me and told me, "You better be nice to God; he is right behind you." When he said that, I ran out of the room in tears and went to the garage and began to cry uncontrollably for a moment.

Then a voice said, *Call Sally and talk to her for a while. She has that calming effect on everyone.* Sally suggested calling Amanda and Latisha and Alison Brennan's mom to come over for help. When Alison came over, she brought the oxygen-level machine. His oxygen level was going up and down; it was like it was all over the page. Also, I put a phone call in to the pharmacy and talked about his pain meds. Come to find out instead of giving him Advil, I was giving him Tylenol, so in turn it was making him worse. After we changed it up, he started to rest better.

I was so grateful for everyone coming over to help me. It was a first; I thought I was really over my head. When George got home, I let him know what went on. His response was, "You're letting him push your buttons." No, this time was different from every time before. I knew the difference between pushing my buttons and not. This was not normal for Luke at all.

The next day was a little better. Luke got up after sleeping in for a while. He wanted his breakfast, and then he wanted to just hang around the house and watch movies for the day. Rob came over to spend a few hours with Luke. It gave us a little time to run to the store to get a few things for dinner. We dropped the groceries home and had a little time before Rob went home.

George and I took a drive out to Lone Tree and gazed out over the water. In the silence, just listening to the water and the calming sound, it is very relaxing and soothing, but my mind wasn't on it. As I looked out the window of the car going over and over in my mind what had happened the night before, tears began to well up in my eyes. As they began to fall, I knew what was starting to unfold. I needed to be strong for Luke. He needed me more than ever before. God gave me the strength that I needed. My heart wept on the inside, but on the outside, the tears never showed. As the edges began to crack, the more strength God gave me.

It's like a balloon that is really stretched before it is about to break. Where it is still pliable, more and more you use your faith. Keep up your trust and the strength will remain. Have courage to go on and face what lies ahead with no questions asked. Just do what your heart directs you to do. It is the right thing to do, and you will have peace and strength all the way through.

Keep believing you did your best. It matters more what is in a person's heart than anything silver or gold can buy. You know what is in a person's heart by the things he or she does. Their actions show what they truly believe.

Luke was always worrying about others, including me. For instance, what would happen to me if something happened to him? God already had it in his plan, somewhere, somehow.

You don't see the plan in the midst of the plan. It is really foggy. You know the time is coming, and you're not ready to face it. More and more, the spinning begins; you don't know from one day to the next. Things happen with no rhyme or reason. In due time, you will know what has taken place. You have to, because the time is getting close for an angel to be called home. Another angel has been brought on board to help gather up the pieces and move forward.

Luke helped in so many ways, helped so many hearts with an encouraging word and a listening ear. He cared enough to hear; he brought great cheer and a few tears. The love we shared with each other and the love that was given, words couldn't express. Our hearts said enough—we didn't have to speak; our hearts spoke for both of us.

The next few nights were the same as Wednesday night. Luke was unable to sleep very well. I called the doctor once again, and again he brought up hospice. We decided to contact them on Monday, since it was already late Friday into Saturday. On Saturday, the oxygen lady came to bring a new device so Luke could have oxygen throughout the house. Luke needed more oxygen during the day as well as at night. We hoped it would help with his comfort level and give him more strength during the day as well.

It broke our hearts more and more each day seeing Luke this way. Each time I would go into his room to adjust him in his bed, I could see he had a scared look in his eyes and wanted me to stay in his room. He didn't want me to leave his side for a minute.

Luke's spirit was strong as his time grew near. It was hard for him to let go. Who was going to take care of his mom when he went home? We'd taken care of and looked after each other for so long; it wasn't going to be the same without the other. We were like best friends. Luke always put others before himself.

Saturday night, Luke was talking to God as he had so many times before. It was that time in the night when you hear quiet voices down the hall as you softly drift off to sleep not knowing what tomorrow will bring. Only the one above knows what it is coming. It's best to live in the moment so that you won't miss a thing when tomorrow comes. You know you did your best with no regrets. Learn from the stepping-stones of yesterday; take what you need and let the rest go. They are the things you can't change.

It was Sunday morning. We got up like it was a regular day, but this day changed in a blink of an eye.

Amanda came to help us get Luke up for the day. As we were talking about what Luke wanted for breakfast and what he wanted to do for the day, all of a sudden Luke's pulse started to race out of control and his breathing started to get real shallow. We called Alison to see if we could use her pulse machine again. Amanda and I ran over to Alison's to get the machine while George stayed home to watch Luke. We put the oxygen on Luke before we left the house so that when we got back, we could check to see if it made a difference. We asked Luke if he wanted to go to the hospital, and he responded no.

When we got home and hooked him up to the machine, his level was going down and down. It went from 80 to 50 in a matter of five minutes. Then his heartbeat kept going down from there. George and I both grabbed the phone at each end of the house and called 911. We were both talking to the EMTs on the phone, and George started doing CPR on Luke. While he was on the phone, they were telling him what to do. It didn't do any good.

God needed Luke with him now, and it was his time to go. Even though it was hard to let him go, God was calling Luke home to make him well, because he couldn't be healed down here. That morning, it took both EMTs twenty minutes to come. Before when we'd called them, they were there in a flash.

It was the day our whole lives changed. It was like a dream you couldn't wake up from. There were so many people there at the house. We talked to the EMTs and the police officers, who knew Luke because he had worked there. They had come to see what had happened. Also, the chief of police came to talk to us and give us his condolences. Talking to others and not remembering talking to them at all . . . it was like I was not there at all. I know in my heart this was the hardest thing in life to do.

I don't care what others think or say about losing a loved one. Losing a child is in a whole different league. It's a club you don't choose to join; it picks you to join. Until you walk into it, this league of your own, you'll never understand. It touches a part of your soul. It's like no other pain you have ever known. You keep searching for answers—*why is this happening to us, and how can I escape from all of this pain?*

It's like going to the mall and your child is lost in the crowd, and you can't seem to find him anywhere. You search high and low, and you keep looking into every child's face thinking you see him. But you are never able to find him. Your mind keeps racing to find understanding. How this could be?

Or you think your child is on a long vacation and he will be home soon. That's how it starts in the beginning, and then as time goes by you find out how real it is, and he's not coming back to us. You trace back the way you remember the time before the final hour when he was called home. You are never ready for such a day and time, but you know it is coming.

Now the day has come, and it is as if you are living outside yourself, and you're just going through the motions. Walking into a room and walking around in circles, not knowing if you are going in or going out. God leads the way and shows you what to do and what needs to be done. He sends people to help you get things prepared to say good-bye for now and let you know he is with you.

Everything is okay, and Luke is in good hands. I heard his voice in my head and my heart: *Keep moving forward one step at a time. Don't worry about me, I am fine. I will be in your hearts forevermore. Remember all the good times we had and all the fun things ahead that God has lined up for you as he has lined up for me in heaven. It is above and beyond anything I had ever dreamed of it to be. I have no more pain or sorrow, no doctors or wheelchairs to adjust forever. As I walked into heaven hand-in-hand with Jesus, as I run through the field of daisies laughing and jumping and having the time of my life, your heart sees more and shows you more if you choose to look close inside. Even if it's hard, it will bring you a little peace of mind each and every day.*

Life is hard, but the way you choose to face it makes a difference. As you go along, it will make a world of difference, the outcome it can bring. Just think about it: what tomorrow may bring in the spring is a gift, not a curse. Each and every one you meet along the way is a gift as well. Everything God gives us is a gift—our talents, our journey, the grand plan he has for each one of us. He loves us all more than we know. The love you receive will remain long after it has been given. Pass it forward to someone else who needs love as well. We see the gifts that were given and the gifts that were left behind.

Luke gave me so much more than money can buy. The gift Luke gave me was his love, the most valuable treasure to give. You can take it wherever you go; it will never tarnish or rust away. The love we share is worth more than silver or gold and can never be stolen or lost. The love you give here on earth to everyone who touches and passes through your life is far more valuable than any treasure. The person who receives love sees a glimpse of God's love and heaven through the love you give.

Once you let a touch of love into your heart, you'll be able to view life in a different way. Each stepping-stone of life happens to you for a reason. You don't know the reasoning at the time. It doesn't make sense until you get through to the other side of the dark tunnel you are in.

Each step you take forms a path each one of us follows each and every day, our blessing from above. Our paths are our own journeys, the stepping-stones of life. Some have smooth edges and some have rough edges. Keep moving forward each day.

CHAPTER 22

What Tomorrow Brings

See what tomorrow brings: a little rain with a glimpse of sunshine. When your heart has been crushed into a million pieces, you find out how real it is when the quiet sets in. When everyone goes home, life goes on for them and you are left alone.

George and I were like two misfits left alone; our lives had been turned upside down and inside out. As time went by, others went on with their own lives like nothing ever happened, and we were left to pick up the pieces, not knowing how to move onward. We just did it.

You try to put on a good front that you'll be okay. But inside, your heart is screaming its head off, as if no one wanted to listen to you. It was as if you were supposed to act like nothing was wrong, not like your world has been turned upside down or anything like that. It made some uncomfortable to be around you or say a word that would upset the cart. No words were spoken.

That's okay. When others leave, new ones come in to share their lives with you once again. Everything changes; nothing stays the same. That's why God gave us a new day to see it in a different way than the one before, to let you know that you are not alone. The love of the angel sent from heaven touched your lives, as well as he did mine.

The story he wants me to tell now, as the clouds start to part and show a glimpse of sunshine through the cracks once again, is that when tomorrow comes—because you know tomorrow always comes— you go through to the other side of tomorrow. You think you are left alone when the darkest hour of grief sets in. Your mind goes haywire, on fire, and out of control. You read into things that don't really exist but seem real at the time. Your loss somehow magnifies everything way out of proportion. You lose your sense of what is right. It is wrong to be thinking that way in the first place, but it is part of your darkest hour that you need to go through.

The darkest hour sets in after everyone goes home and you think you are left alone. But you're not left alone at all. God is with you. He helps you through the dark moments each and every day. It becomes lighter as each day the sun comes up. All you have to do is ask; he will be there with his arms open wide.

When you try to do it on your own, it only gets worse. Or you try to bury it and come back to it and deal with the pain at a much later time. When you put it off, the darker it becomes, until everything around you begins to escalate out of control and you hit bottom.

When you don't deal with things head on, you begin to blame others for all the pain that you're not ready to face. That was the case for us; each one of us faced grief in different ways and different stages in the midst of the wilderness that we were all in.

One shoots to anger and the other needs comfort and understanding. Some need to go to their own corners for a little while until they feel safe to come out and connect with each other once again. Some choose to run away, and that isn't the answer either, because it will follow you wherever you go. There is no escaping it but to go through it. Work through as you learn to adjust to what has taken place as you face another day. Give yourself time to listen to your little voice deep inside. It will comfort and guide you to get you to where you need to be—on to where you are going from here, the steps that you need to take.

Even when it doesn't make sense at the time, just know that voice will never steer you wrong, it is always right. Even though your feelings haven't caught up yet, listen to the peaceful voice that comes back. *I will be with you every step of the way. I have been with you since the beginning, and I will see you through till the end.* Keep believing and hoping, and you will slowly see your life turn around right in front of you.

Trust God, and he will make it better in time. That's God's timing, not yours. His time is right. It really works when you take your time and slow down. God knows what we need before we even ask for it, but he still wants us to ask. When you ask, he knows that you're ready to face it full steam ahead. Sometimes it means starting from the beginning once again, to show us where all the anger started, buried deep inside. It has reached the surface, and now the lid has been removed—like a pop can that has been shaken so much that the top has popped off, spraying all over the one it is pointed at.

Now it is time to deal with your anger that has been buried deep inside. It is time to let it fly out and let it go once and for all. Once you face your fears or your past hurts, your healing begins. Your breakthrough is underway.

Break away from your old habits to make room for the new and wonderful you. It is a daily process to chip away all the pieces of the wall that was built one stone at a time. Let go of what lies behind so you can focus on what lies ahead of you—the real unique and divine you that you need to see come out and shine, the one buried deep inside of you. You take bits and pieces, what you learned each and every day, some good and some bad, to lead you to where you are and then back home someday.

We have to follow Jesus' example, as Luke did his whole life, one day at a time. The story he left behind for others to hear; the race he ran and won. He touched and changed others through all the love he gave during his life.

We celebrated Luke going home to be with Jesus. It was a revelation to me when Pastor Scott said Luke was a window to God. The light came on for me, how blessed we really are and how grateful that God let us be a part of an awesome gift. I'm sharing my gift with you, a story of a little boy who touched me. He touched my heart in such a way that I will never be the same. I got to see into his heart, the real deal, as he did mine. I got to see God walk beside me through Luke's life journey.

The day Luke was laid to rest, I asked God to show me a sign that Luke was with him. He showed us two. The first one: It was really cold that day and the wind was blowing. Then all of a sudden, the sun broke and the warm sun shined down on the NASCAR casket. The warmth of the sunshine reflected on our faces. We asked others if they saw what we had seen, and the answer was no. The second one: As we released the balloons, they started racing toward the crack into the sky. A few popped, letting off a sound to let you know he made it home. As you glanced into the sky a little closer, it was Jesus as his face appeared in the clouds to let us know Luke was where he was supposed to be now and he was okay.

The way you walk in love that impacts others is what you leave behind. It shows you what things matter and what things do not. Luke showed us real love, which matters most of all. It showed through the way he lived and the real love he left behind. After reading his story, you will see life in a different light that each and every day is a gift from heaven above, just as Luke viewed his life to be a blessing no matter how he felt and how many obstacles he was up against. Some were a lot harder than others, but he faced each and every one. We all have obstacles, but how you view them is up to you. They can hold you back or you can face them full speed ahead as Luke did and never give up.

Luke lived his life to the fullest, and always with a smile on his face. Luke won his race; he got into the winner's circle he always dreamed of, with his winner's cup and his checkered flags flying in the wind, with his flowers and his racecar shining with fresh paint and gauges that show his speed and special pictures in the winner's circle with all the red carpet.

We played music with your winning lap, Luke, and showed all the pictures of days gone by, to remember each day you're in heaven driving your very own shiny racecar specially made just for you. We see the smile upon your face, lit up for miles. The day of the race and your the winning run. The race is won now that you are home.

CHAPTER 23

A Letter Home

Dear Mom and Dad,
I know you love and miss me
just as I love and miss you
since, I went away.
Just remember it is only for a little while.
One day we will be reunited, in our father's house
we will be in heaven.
I am with you still in your heart, every day shining bright.
I am your angel in flight.
I received my special wings,
my coat sparkling white,
My mansion on the hill with sparkling gold walkways,
and field full of daisies all around is laughter all day long to enjoy.
So don't worry; I am fine, no more tears.
Remember me and the happy times we shared
And all the memories that remain.
Take care.
Love only remains and joy will return.
Love ya always, Luke

THINGS I'VE LEARNED FROM LUKE'S LIFE

I've learned so much about Luke's life—how close God was to us the whole time. Even when you don't think he is near, he is a lot closer than you think. Keep the faith and you will see for yourself how to forgive others and yourself for all the hurts and pains, to let things go from the past you can't change anyway.

Why fret over the past? The past is the past. Learn from your mistakes. Follow those stepping-stones toward what lies ahead of you. You need to, because the future God has planned for you is so amazing. He will help you steer through the pain of all that darkness, and a glimpse of light each day you will begin to see. It is there when you look up and take notice. Take each step one at a time. Grab hold and he'll lead you through the rough and rocky road ahead of you. You have to put your trust and faith in him, knowing he will be with you every step of the way.

Others may just walk away, but he will never walk away from you. He is by your side even when you feel like you're alone, but know you will never be alone with God on your side. He always keeps his promises even when others let you down. He will never let you down. He always follows through with his promises, each and every one.

Know that he is with you every step of the way. It's not easy to take that first step, but it is worth the progress I've made to get to the other side. As I look back over my journey, the real love was revealed once my heart was broken, and it is in the process of being made whole again. Through the love from the little angel who was called home, the gifts he gave, we got to bear witness to a loving and caring soul. He saved me in so many ways. He was sent to show God's love through himself. You are able to know him by the way he lived and loved as if you met him face to face. He lived his life to the fullest, always with a smile on his face.

Throughout Luke's life, he had a lot of courage and strength, and he shared his love with everyone he met along the way. For those who didn't get to meet Luke, I hope I have given you a glimpse of how special he was. We will see each other again someday. Keep running your race.

Thanks, Luke, for all you have done in my life, for the love you gave without even knowing it and all the lives you touched with soft-spoken words. You will be dearly missed. You will never be forgotten. You will live forevermore in our hearts. When we say your name, we see your smiling face looking back at us, comfortable knowing you are up in heaven with Jesus.

Luke, I envision you every day running through the field of daises and laughing and jumping having fun. Life can never be shaken with our angels up above watching over us, here and everywhere through our journey each and every day. The love we shared is the love you left behind to be shared with the ones you have not passed by yet.

Remember me until we meet again in heaven when my journey's over. Love, Mom

Closing Thoughts Between a Mother and Son

You did the best you could, and that's all that matters to me.
Give yourself permission to keep moving forward.
Thank you for being my son and loving me the way you did—
Just the way you loved me.
Don't be afraid. God and I will be with you every step of the way.
Start today and do what's in your heart.

Notes from the heart . . .
Remember . . .
God was with us the day you were born.
God was with us the day he took you home, to make you well again.
I know where you are—
Where there is no more pain or rain falling down.
Heaven rejoices with another angel returning home;
Laughing and running and jumping and having fun.
It is sad down here without you here with us.
But knowing where you are makes it a little easier,
knowing we will be together soon.
When feeling blue, I shut my eyes and see you
running through a field of daisies,
Laughing and giggling and standing up straight,
and you are having a grand time.
It makes my heart feel a sense of joy flow through.
Then my day seems a little brighter, as you speak
to my heart and say it will be okay.
We will see each other again someday. You
reassure me to keep running my race.
That's my gift to you.
I will walk beside you.

Deann holding Luke as a baby "Hot afternoon"

Luke sleeping softly

Luke's 1st Birthday

Luke chillin on the couch

Luke in sailor suit—Halloween

Luke standing on his own "Awesome"

Luke sitting on his three wheeler

George and Deann and Luke sitting hanging out

Deann and Luke and George "Sweetness"

George and Luke and Deann "Precious"

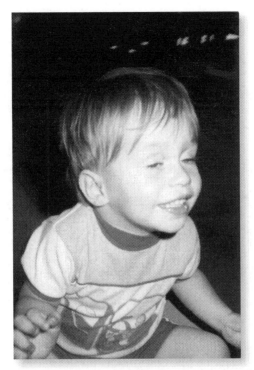

Luke

Luke at 3yrs and Latisha new born "Brotherly Love"

Luke and Latisha in rocker

Luke's smile that lasts for miles

Luke holding "Beans"

Luke and Latisha and "Mr. Snow Man"

Luke and Santa

Luke and Latisha in Santa hats

Luke and Latisha back from "DisneyLand 1991"

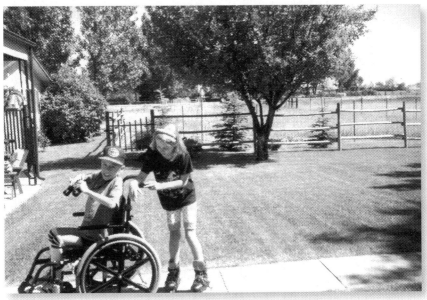

Luke and Latisha "Having Fun"

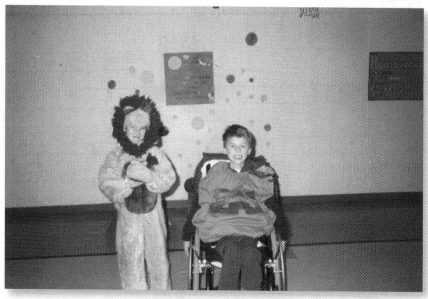

Luke and Latisha "Halloween"

Luke and George "The catch of the day"

George and Luke smiles "Burn Bright what a delight"

Luke fishing "Waiting"

George and Luke and Latisha at Disneyland

Luke Christmas day

Luke enjoying the shade

Tom and Luke and Brennan at the ball game

Luke with friends at camp

The whole family "Luke's Graduation"

Luke and Latisha "Latisha 18th Birthday party"

Luke and Auston "Proud uncle full of Love"

George and Deann

Luke and Michael "Friends"

Denise and Alison and Luke "Memories"

Luke at the House